"Bert Ghezzi is recognized as a p
ful author. His most recent work,
provides helpful insight into what ......... as our
conversation with God. This engaging book is rooted in sacred
Scripture and our Catholic tradition, and should serve as an
inspiration to many people who strive to enrich their prayer
life."

—**Cardinal Donald W. Wuerl, STD,**
Archbishop of Washington

"Bert Ghezzi brings the tradition home to this generation.
Through his books he has helped us to know the saints, know
the sacraments, know the cross—and know ourselves as we
stand before God. When Bert writes about Catholic matters,
they seem self-evident. He brings lofty truths down to earth."

—**Scott Hahn,** author of *The Lamb's Supper*
and *Rome Sweet Home*

"Another great book by Bert Ghezzi! In this book, Bert once
again takes a common-sense approach to guiding people in their
relationships with God. He uses many of his own experiences
to illustrate how praying is more natural than breathing. If you
want to grow in your spiritual life, read this book, implement
some of its suggestions, and you will be on your way."

—**Fr. Larry Richards,** founder,
The Reason for Our Hope Foundation;
pastor, St. Joseph Church Bread of Life Community

"This is a fine little book, wise and tender and filled with grace."

—**Dean Koontz,** bestselling suspense novelist

"At the risk of seeming to have engaged in an extravagant state-
ment, I still venture to say that not one of us presently writing
about religion in this country is better equipped by experience,

skill, and devotion to write about prayer than Bert Ghezzi. He lives what he speaks, and he speaks what he lives very, very well."

—**Phyllis Tickle**, author of *Prayer Is a Place*
and *The Great Emergence*

"When we pray, we join a chorus of voices from all Christian traditions that harmoniously transcend our denominational differences. Bert Ghezzi has given us a practical guide to voice lessons for those who want to raise their hearts to God. Impeccably researched, authentically lived, and engagingly written, this guide will appeal to Catholics and Protestants alike. I could not recommend a book—or a person—more highly."

—**Ken Gire**, author, *Moments with the Savior*,
*Windows of the Soul*, and *The Weathering Grace of God*

"In *The Power of Daily Prayer*, Bert Ghezzi answers the questions we all have about how and why we should pray via his own lifelong prayer journey. Readers will be grateful for this helpful and engaging book."

—**Amy Welborn**, author of *The Words We Pray:*
*Discovering the Richness of Catholic Prayer*

"Bert Ghezzi has written yet another superb book to help us become people of deeper prayer. Bert opens not only the treasures of the church but also the treasures of his own heart. I feel challenged and encouraged by *The Power of Daily Prayer* and you will too. No matter where you are in your own journey with God, this book will inspire you to grow!"

—**Patti Gallagher Mansfield**, leader of Catholic Charismatic
Renewal; author of *As By a New Pentecost*

# *The* POWER *of* DAILY PRAYER

### Also by Bert Ghezzi

*Voices of the Saints*

*The Saints Devotional Bible (NABRE)*

*Discover Christ* (with Dave Nodar)

*Breakfast with Benedict* (compiler/editor)

*Everyday Encounters with God*
   (with Benedict Groeschel, CFR)

*Saints at Heart*

*Living the Sacraments*

*The Sign of the Cross*

*Mystics and Miracles*

*Getting Free*

# *The* POWER *of* DAILY PRAYER

## BERT GHEZZI

theWORD among us® Press

Published in 2013 by The Word Among Us Press
7115 Guilford Road
Frederick, Maryland 21704
www.wau.org

18 17 16 15 14    2 3 4 5 6
ISBN: 978-1-59325-246-5

Cover design by Koechel Peterson & Associates

Library of Congress Control Number: 2013940481

For my sons and daughters and their families

John, Paul, Elaine, Stephen, Peter, Clare, and Mary

# Contents

"Acquire the habit of speaking to God as if you were alone with God. Speak with familiarity and confidence as to your dearest and most loving friend. Speak of your life, your plans, your troubles, your joys, your fears. In return, God will speak to you—not that you will hear audible words in your ears, but words that you will clearly understand in your heart."[1]

—St. Alphonsus de'Liguori (1696–1797)

# Introduction

This year my friend Fr. Gene celebrated the fiftieth anniversary of his ordination as a priest. During his long ministry he has heard the confessions of thousands of women and men. He has given spiritual direction to hundreds of others. He says that in one-on-one sessions people have always wanted to talk about important matters, such as family, careers, sex, sickness, and death. But you may be surprised to learn—as I was—that the topic people raised most frequently by far was prayer. Most said that they were trying to pray and wanted to learn how to do it better.

Father Gene's experience should not really have surprised me. Americans put a high priority on prayer. Surveys consistently show that the vast majority of us pray frequently. Ninety percent pray at least once a week and 59 percent pray daily. I would not have predicted the following statistic. The Pew Research Center reports that "less than one-third

(32%) of men under age 30 say they attend church weekly. But 83% of these younger men pray on a weekly basis, and 43% say they pray daily."[1] They may have drifted away from church, but they have stayed close to God through prayer.

We have many good reasons to pray. We intercede for the present and ultimate well-being of our family, our friends, our nation, the world, and ourselves. A daughter gives birth to twins prematurely. A lovely neighbor slides into dementia. A favorite uncle with terminal cancer asks us to pray with him for a peaceful death and his heavenly repose. Our company is downsizing and we must find a new job. Millions suffer without food and water. Climate change threatens to wreak havoc on earth. We take these and like concerns to God.

We also pray for our daily needs. The car breaks down, the water heater bursts, and we are anticipating the inevitable third disaster of the week. We ask God for help with such mundane affairs.

We offer thanks, too, for blessings. Grandma visits and occupies the toddlers for a week. An alcoholic son celebrates five years of sobriety. We write the check that pays off our credit card debt. Graces such as these nudge us to express our gratitude to God.

Sometimes just enjoying the wonders of creation drives us to our knees. A sparkling evening sky reminds us that one hundred billion galaxies—each with one hundred billion stars—swirl above us. A crape myrtle that we thought had died resurrects and explodes with delicate blossoms. We view hi-tech photographs of a two-month-old fetus—no bigger than a grape—that has all its major organs in place and ready to develop. Awe at God's handiwork leads to adoration.

And like St. Richard of Chichester (ca. 1197–1253), we may simply turn to the Lord expressing our desire to know him more clearly, love him more dearly, and follow him more nearly.[2] Or like Jesus himself—St. Richard's model and ours—we may often slip away to a quiet place where we can commune with our Father.

These prayers flow from the depths of our hearts, but beneath them God himself stirs us. He surrounds us with his love and invites us to spend time with him. He brings us into a relationship with him so that we can get to know him. He has made us his friends.

Even before we may be aware of it, the Lord engages us in an adventure of prayer. Moment by moment he beckons us, creating opportunities for us to communicate with him. All prayer rises up in us as God's gift. He is coming to us more than we are going to him. The classic Baltimore Catechism popularized the definition of prayer as "raising the mind and heart to God." Jesuit spiritual writer Thomas H. Green (1932–2009) says that this description goes too far because it makes it seem as though we are initiators of the communication. Alternatively, he suggests that we characterize prayer as "opening the mind and heart to God" because the idea of "opening" emphasizes responsiveness and receptivity.[3] Whether we are beginners, experienced pray-ers, or "in-betweeners," we are always the recipients of God's gift of prayer.

In these pages I share in detail my experiencees of daily prayer. I offer them as a series of mirrors in which you can reflect on your own prayer life. I will tell of the ways the Lord has worked in me so they may trigger your memories of the ways he has worked in you. Each chapter explains an element that characterizes my prayer times—practices such as living in God's presence, listening to God, and interceding for others. In order to help you connect with my message and explore its value for you, I have provided Think, Pray, and Act questions at the end of each chapter. You may also use these questions—especially those labeled "Think"—for group discussions.

I began to receive the gift of prayer fifty years ago. And I still welcome it every day. I describe the then and now of my prayer life in the first chapter.

# 1

## The Gift of Daily Prayer

I learned to pray among friends at Duquesne University in Pittsburgh, Pennsylvania. Early in 1959, my freshman year, I bumped into some students who gathered for morning prayers before classes. They invited me to join them, and I did. So began my adventures in daily prayer.

Before that time I had a casual attitude toward prayer, typical of cradle Catholics in the 1950s. My dad died of a heart attack when I was twelve. My mother, a devout Catholic, raised my three siblings and me as a single parent. We prayed grace before meals, but not after. As a teenager I abandoned bedtime prayers, which I regarded as childish. The family attended Sunday worship, but we never prayed together at home. At the parish school I learned the classic prayers and prayed them with my fellows at the appointed times during the school day. Occasionally I prayed them on my own, but not very often. Although my experience of prayer during these years was su-

---

**A Vocabulary for Living Godward**

Still today the Old Testament book of Psalms gives great power for faith and life. This is simply because it preserves a conceptually rich language about God and our relationships to him. If you bury yourself in Psalms, you emerge knowing God and understanding life.

And that is by no means a matter, as some suggest, of the "poetic effect" of the great language. No mere emotional lift is involved. What makes the language great and provides the emotional lift is chiefly its picture of God and of life. We learn from the psalms how to think and act in reference to God. We drink in God and God's world from them. They provide a vocabulary for living Godward, one inspired by God himself. They show us who God is, and that expands and lifts and directs our minds and hearts.

—Dallas Willard, *The Divine Conspiracy*[1]

---

perficial, my immersion in the traditional piety of my parish and schools somewhat prepared me for what was to come. I had acquired a textbook knowledge about sacraments, saints, sanctifying grace, and, of course, firsthand knowledge about sin—but not about Scripture. That would come later.

## Learning to Pray

At Duquesne I quickly got into the spirit of daily morning prayer. I joined Dorothy, Jack, Josie, Don, Lorraine, Bob, and others who were also learning to pray. We met at 8 a.m. sharp in the department of history offices, which were located in an old house at the center of campus. On cold winter mornings ancient radiators banged as they warmed up and provided a percussion accompaniment to our prayers. Professor William G. Storey, now a renowned historian of the liturgy, led our morning worship. He was developing a layperson's version of the liturgy of the hours, the official prayer of the church that priests and religious men and women pray daily. Later published as *Morning Praise and Evensong,* it became very popular in the years after the Second Vatican Council. He piloted mimeographed copies of the text with us at our morning prayer.

Patterned on the hours, *Morning Praise and Evensong* contained hymns, prayers, antiphons, psalms, canticles, and Scripture arranged in an orderly structure. We stood in a circle, sang the hymn, prayed the psalms and canticles antiphonally, and took turns reading the prayers and the Scripture lesson.

The experience was life changing. I learned many things about God, prayer, and myself. For example, I discovered the value of right postures at prayer and of the ancient Christian gestures long embedded in Catholic tradition. Standing erect, making the sign of the cross, folding hands, striking the breast, bowing at the doxology, listening attentively, and practicing silence at appropriate moments all taught me reverence. I sensed that by attuning my body to prayer I was honoring the Lord with my whole being.

More than anything else, those morning gatherings taught me how to pray. The psalms tutored me. They flooded my mind with images that revealed the greatness of the Lord. I prayed to the God who "counts out the number of the stars, and gives each one of them a name" (Ps. 147:4 NJB). I addressed the God whose thoughts, if I had enough time to count them, would total more than all the grains of sand on every shore (see Ps. 139:18). Psalm 145 and others like it showed me why God deserved my praise and thanks and gave me the words with which to offer them:

> I will exalt you, my God the King:
> > I will praise your name for ever and ever.
> Great is the LORD and most worthy of praise;
> > his greatness no one can fathom.
> The LORD is gracious and compassionate,

17

slow to anger and rich in love.
The LORD upholds all those who fall
    and lifts up all who are bowed down.
You open your hand
    and satisfy the desires of every living thing.
The LORD is near to all who call on him,
to all who call on him in truth.
                    —Psalm 145:1, 3, 8, 14, 16, 18 NIV

Praying with psalms as a young man shaped my prayer life by positioning me before God as he revealed himself. I feel that they helped me thwart a temptation described in the wonderful *Screwtape Letters* by C. S. Lewis (1898–1963). At one point Screwtape, a master devil, instructs a demon trainee to tempt his victim to pray to a god that he imagines, and thus not to God at all. Screwtape says that if the victim ever consciously directs his prayers to God as he reveals himself—instead of his imagined god—then the tempter's situation becomes desperate. "Once all his thoughts and images have been flung aside . . . and the man trusts himself to the completely real, external, invisible Presence, there with him in the room . . . why, then it is that the incalculable may occur."[2] So praying psalms prevented me from worshiping a god that I might have created in my imagination—perhaps a cruel, vengeful god or a distant, uncaring one. Immersing myself in the psalms caused me to worship God as he is.

### How I Pray Now

Five decades later I still begin every day with prayer. I settle in my living room with a cup of coffee, my Bible, prayer book, and books for spiritual reading. In the quiet of the early morning I find it easy to re-collect myself. I begin by acknowledging God's presence. I know that the creator of the unimaginably vast and beautiful universe is my constant companion. But I remain unaware of God's closeness until I remind myself that he is always with me, eager to engage me in conversation.

I also begin my morning prayer by remembering that I am not praying alone. I recognize that I am joining a wonderful chorus that echoes throughout the universe, honoring God with praise and thanksgiving. I unite my prayer with this worship offered within the communion of saints, the prayer of angels and of women and men who have gone before me to the heavenly kingdom. Sometimes I call on them by name, linking my words with those of well-known saints like Teresa of Avila (1515–82) and Thomas More (1477–1535), and with those of some lesser known favorites of mine like Anne-Marie Javouhey (1779–1851), and Aelred of Rievaulx (1110–67). On this earthly side of the communion of saints, I also join with the prayer of William Storey, my friend and mentor, and that of my other early-bird friends.

So once God has my attention, I am ready for him to begin the conversation. He has been waiting patiently to communicate with me. I listen quietly and let him lead my prayer. Sometimes he draws me to a psalm, a Scripture text, or a prayer like the *Hymn to the Holy Spirit*, which I carry on a card in my Bible. So I pray the ancient hymn:

> Holy Spirit, font of light,
>> focus of God's glory bright,
>> shed on us a shining ray.
> Father of the fatherless,
>> giver of gifts limitless,

come and touch our hearts today.
Source of strength and sure relief,
   comforter in times of grief,
      enter in and be our guest.
On our journey grant us aid,
   freshening breeze and cooling shade,
      in our labor inward rest.
Enter each aspiring heart,
   occupy its inmost part
      with your dazzling purity.
All that gives to us our worth,
   all that benefits the earth,
      you bring to maturity.
With your soft refreshing rains
   break our drought, remove our stains;
      bind up all our injuries.
Shake with rushing wind our will;
   melt with fire our icy chill;
      bring to light our perjuries.
As your promise we believe,
   make us ready to receive
      gifts from your unbounded store.
Grant enabling energy,
   courage in adversity,
      joys that last forever more.[3]

I never pray these words casually, for I know the Spirit does what this hymn asks of him. I pray it expecting him to act in my life during the day. He may give me just the right words to encourage a friend who did not get the promotion he expected.

Or he may urge me to help an out-of-work friend make his rent payment. I count on the Spirit to guide me to do the right thing.

On some mornings the Holy Spirit directs my thoughts either to the core of my sinfulness or to the wisdom he is giving me for my spiritual journey. So I open my prayer by asking God to help me surrender more fully to him. On other mornings I am led to open my prayer with a litany of thanksgiving. I thank him for all the wonderful things he has done. For such big things as the creation of the universe, this earth as a dwelling for billions of people made in his image, and sending his Son to redeem us. And I praise him for his uncountable kindnesses to me, especially family, friends, and forgiveness. Realizing what God has done for me makes me love him all the more.

After such times of informal conversations with God, I take up my prayer book. I now use *A Catholic Book of Hours and Other Devotions*,[4] Dr. Storey's most recent version of the liturgy of the hours for laypeople. I still pray morning prayer, as I did so many years ago at Duquesne. I like it because it is more than mere formal prayer. Like the Mass, the morning hour is part of the liturgy, which is the prayer Christ as head of the church

---

**Unlock the Door of Your Soul**

Let your door stand open to receive [Christ], unlock your soul to him, offer him a welcome in your mind, and then you will see the riches of simplicity, the treasures of peace, the joy of grace. Throw wide the gate of your heart, stand before the sun of the everlasting light *that shines on every man*. This true light shines on all, but if anyone closes his window he will deprive himself of eternal light. If you shut the door of your mind, you shut out Christ. Though he can enter, he does not want to force his way in rudely, or compel us to admit him against our will.

—Exposition on Psalm 118 by St. Ambrose (339–97) in
*The Office of Readings According to the Roman Rite*[5]

---

prays with and through its members. Praying morning prayer allows me to join the cosmic prayer of Christ himself. So I am not praying idle words. Rather I am uniting my heart with the Lord's heart, preparing myself in the morning to collaborate throughout the day with him in his ministry to humankind. I am absorbing the grace I will need to respond with kindness to everyone I meet.

At some point during my morning worship, I read a portion of Scripture. I try to figure out what the Bible writer was saying to his original readers. I reflect on what I think the text means for my life. Sometimes I take away from a book an overall impression that supports my spiritual life. When I read Genesis, for example, and realize that God achieved his purposes with flawed people, I gain confidence that he may be able to accomplish something with me despite my faults.

All during my prayer time I try to hear what the Lord is saying to me. I take time to listen to him, paying attention to the main thoughts that he seems to impress on me. A line from a psalm may strike me as his word for the day. Sometimes he gives me an assurance that he is taking care of a family matter that concerns me. He may direct me to pray for a sick neighbor or about an issue at work. He may bring someone to mind that he wants me to speak to. I frequently ask the Lord what he wants me to do with my life either short term or long term. In a notebook, I keep track of what the Lord seems to be saying to me.

Every morning I conclude my prayer with intercessions. I pray for family, relatives, friends, neighbors, colleagues, and casual acquaintances. Although I pray for specific things, such as healing, freedom from an addiction, or success at some venture, I ask the Holy Spirit to intercede as well. He knows better than I do what the people I am praying for need most. I especially pray

22

for my wife, my children, and grandchildren. I tell the Lord that I want all of us to be together in heaven. I believe he just can't say no to a dad's prayer for his family's salvation.

I wrap up with a short prayer. Then I grab a second cup of coffee and am ready to tackle whatever comes that day.

In this picture of my morning prayer time I have described key elements that help me open to the Lord. Coming into God's presence, immersion in the Holy Spirit, reflecting on Scripture, listening to God, and interceding with faith are not just my idiosyncratic practices. They characterize all Christian prayer and are normal habits of all prayers. As such, these practices combine to create robust daily prayer times. I plan to explore each of them in the chapters that follow.

Think
- What role has prayer played in your life?
- Why do you pray?
- How often do you pray?

Pray
Take fifteen minutes to pray. Consider these questions:

- Recall a time or times when you wanted to pray. In what ways do you think the Lord prompted your desire to pray?
- What do you expect God to do when you pray?

Act
- Pray all verses of Psalm 145 once each day for a week.
- After a week, make a list of what you have learned from the psalm about God and about yourself.

# 2

## Giving Ourselves to God

The participants in the Duquesne morning prayer group gradually developed into an informal community. Praying together forged strong bonds of friendship among us. We also discovered that we shared many common concerns. We wanted to learn more about prayer, theology, and Scripture than were being taught in the university curriculum. The announcement by Pope John XXIII (1881–1963) of his intention to convoke an ecumenical council awakened our hope for church reform and liturgical renewal, especially the promise of worship in the vernacular. In order to pursue these interests, we formed ourselves into a campus society. We positioned the group as a religious fraternity by calling it Chi Rho, the first two letters of Christ's name in Greek.

I loved our morning prayers and came to regard them as a highlight of my school day. Our study of Catholic spirituality at Chi Rho meetings impressed on me that personal prayer was just as important as communal worship. As a faithful Jew, Jesus participated in family prayer with his parents, in his local synagogue, and in the communal prayer of the temple. He prayed with his disciples as well. But he also taught us to pray to God simply in the privacy of our rooms (see Matt. 5:6–7). I observed in the Gospels that Jesus regularly spent personal time with his Father. In Luke I read that sometimes after caring for the crowds he would slip away to a deserted place or climb a mountain to pray (see Luke 5:15; 6:12).

Sometime during my sophomore year I made a commitment to take a daily prayer time. Every night for about fifteen minutes before or after studying I prayed classic Catholic prayers mixed with spontaneous words of thanks and petition. Or I prayed the psalms from *Morning Praise and Evensong*. Daily prayer proved to be habit forming. Over the years I varied my prayers. I prayed longer and at different times and places. My circumstances changed many times, but I have managed to keep my commitment. Investing time in daily prayer has produced incalculable rewards for me. Regular prayer times gave me continuous opportunities to enjoy God's love and to sustain my friendship with him.

## Regular Prayer

As savvy consumers we are familiar with optional extras. When I purchased my laptop, Dell offered me a variety of options, including a microphone, web camera, gaming accessories, graphic and editing software, and an extended warranty. Hyundai tantalized Mary Lou, my wife, with a moon roof and a GPS device for her new Sonata. We both bypassed the optional extras and stuck to the essentials. I wanted a hard drive with enough data storage capacity and speed to handle my daily work. Although I joke that Mary Lou chooses a car based on the number of cup holders, she really made her choice by consulting consumer magazines on the basics. While bells and whistles have some appeal, the true value of a computer or car lies in its function and reliability.

We must approach our spirituality the same way. Regular prayer is an essential element of Christian living, not an optional extra such as occasionally attending a lecture or concert. Praying daily is the hard drive that makes our Christian life work, the engine that drives our spiritual growth. Without it our relationship with God founders and our Christian life sputters and drifts.

In the gift exchange that we call Christianity, God created us to be his children and sealed his relationship with us by sending his only Son to gather us and bring us into his kingdom (see Eph. 1:1–14). Saint Peter says that he not only lavishes on us everything we need for life and true devotion, but he also fulfills his priceless promises by sharing his divine nature with us (see 2 Pet. 1:3–4). Words like "gigantic" or "cosmic" cannot describe the enormity of his wondrous gift. The human mind with all its marvelous capabilities cannot conceive it. The eternal, self-existent, infinitely powerful, wise, and perfect God who created everything from nothing and sustains all creation loves us, chases us down, and presents himself to us as a gift.

We respond to God's generosity by offering him our whole being—body, mind, and spirit. That's all we have to give, but that's all God wants. Remember how Jesus praised the poor widow who contributed two pennies—all she had—to the temple treasury (see Mark 12:43). Similarly we participate in the great exchange by giving our all to him. So God engages us in a dynamic relationship. Our friendship with him matures

### The Stuff of Intimacy with God

Ordinary chitchat [for example with our mother] is not the stuff of intimacy, but regular contact is because, as the chitchat is going on, something deeper is happening . . . under the surface. This is also true of our prayer lives and our relationship with God. If we make a commitment to sit in private prayer every day for half an hour, how many times might we expect that we'll feel a deep movement of soul, a stunning insight, or an affirmation that really warms us? A dozen times a year? Five or six times a year? Perhaps.

Most of the time though our prayer time will be a lot like those visits we make regularly to our mothers . . . We will treasure those times when something special breaks through, but those times will not be what's really important. What's really important will be what's growing under the surface, namely, a bond and an intimacy that's based upon a familiarity that can only develop and sustain itself by regular contact, by actually sharing life on a day-to-day basis.

—Ronald Rolheiser[1]

as we come to know and love him more. Daily prayer is the place where this exchange of gifts takes place.

## A Time and a Place

For the past quarter century I have had no difficulty finding a time and place to pray. I take my prayer time first thing in the morning at my usual spot in our living room. Praying in that corner for so many years seems to have hallowed it. I station myself at my favorite chair with my Bible and prayer books at hand, and the space itself invites me to turn to the Lord.

I am a very early riser, always the first one up in our family. At a pre-dawn hour the house is quiet. In the stillness I find it easy to open my mind and heart to God. I have always been alert and productive in the morning. I enjoy reserving the best part of that prime time for pursuing my relationship with the Lord. Mary Lou, however, is not a morning person. As is the case for many people, her prime time occurs in the evening, and that's when she prays.

It has not always been so easy for me to find a time to pray. From my student days through career and job changes, I have had to overcome many obstacles to keep my commitment to daily prayer. Finding time for uninterrupted prayer in an ever-changing, busy schedule presented the greatest challenge.

My worst prayer experience occurred in the late 1960s when I was teaching history at Grand Valley State College (now University) near Grand Rapids, Michigan. Faced with an overload of commitments, I schemed to simplify things. I decided to pray while I drove the twenty-five miles from my home in Grand Haven, Michigan, to the college. Daily I sped along state road M 45, praying and singing as the lovely countryside zipped by. Then one day flashing red and blue lights abruptly distracted me from my reverie. The state trooper who pulled me over said, "Young man, do you realize you were doing seventy-five miles an hour in a twenty-five-mile-an-hour zone?" I was tempted to defend myself by saying something like, "Sir, you must understand that I was caught up in prayer and lost track of earthly things." But I wisely kept my mouth shut. My folly cost me a seventy-five dollar fine, a high price to pay on a monthly salary of seven hundred dollars—even for a great prayer time. The moral of the story: don't pray and drive.

Resolved not to pray behind the wheel, I began the next day to take my prayer time at a church on my route to work. Except for the disastrous mobile prayer episode, finding places to pray never presented much of a problem. As a student, I prayed in my room; newly married, I used a spare bedroom in the apartment; in four different family homes, I made a place in the living room; and in two work situations I prayed in vacant offices.

**Jesus Shared Our Struggles with Prayer**

Jesus had the same trouble finding time to pray that we have. He was not a first-century superman—able to go without food or sleep in a way that we ourselves cannot...Therefore, when Jesus spent the whole night in prayer, he had to sacrifice sleep and battle fatigue, just as we would have to do. When Jesus rose early in the morning to pray, it took resolve on his part, a determination to make time for communion with his Father . . .

If we must contend with erratic schedules and the demands of family life, Jesus had to contend with even greater demands. If the pace of modern life seems too rapid to allow us the luxury of prayer, the public ministry of Jesus was no less hectic. If we have trouble finding a quiet place to be alone with God, Jesus experienced the same difficulty. If our work demands much of us, Jesus' ministry demanded no less of him.

—George Martin, *Praying with Jesus*[2]

Extreme busyness, excessive commitments, and family responsibilities made finding time for prayer a recurring problem. As a student the press of assignments and deadlines required me to approach prayer more fluidly than was good for my spiritual well-being. I sometimes had to pray at night when I tended to enter an altered state of exhaustion, not to be mistaken for ecstasy. After babies arrived, Mary Lou and I covered for each other, one caring for the toddlers while the other prayed. At two different companies, demanding work schedules called for creative tactics. I used breaks or lunch times for prayer and enlisted vigilant secretaries to protect me from interruptions. My struggle to find a time and place for prayer ended when I moved to Florida in 1985 and launched the early morning routine that I have enjoyed for twenty-five years running.

We need to pray daily as our response to God's outrageous, extravagant love for us. Think about it. He had us in mind as his companions before he created anything. Then he unfolded this vast universe of a hundred billion trillion stars so that on this lovely little planet he could enjoy friendship with you and me.

Imagine what we are missing of God's lavish affection if we just pray when we feel like it. Or if we just try to pray daily, but too often find something else to do. Regular prayer holds up our side of the relationship. It affirms our friendship with the Lord, our commitment to love him with all our heart, mind, and strength.

Think
- Have you made a commitment to pray regularly?
- Do you have a place where you can pray uninterrupted?
- Do you pray at a regular time?
- What obstacles might be hindering your practice of regular prayer? What can you do to overcome them?

Pray
Take fifteen minutes to pray. Consider these questions:

- If you have a commitment to pray daily, have you been faithful to do it? What would it take for you to renew your commitment?
- If you have not made a commitment to daily prayer, what steps could you take to do it now?

Act
- Pray the *Hymn to the Holy Spirit* (chap. 1, pp. 19–20) every day for a week.
- At the end of the week, write down what the Holy Spirit seems to be saying to you about your prayer life.

# 3

## Living in God's Presence

Acknowledging that the Lord is with me is the first thing I do when I pray. I do not try to feel his presence, but I make myself aware that God himself is waiting to talk with me. It is like looking up from a book I'm reading and noticing that a friend who has entered the room is waiting to catch my attention. "Oh, I'm glad you've dropped by," I say. "Sit down and let's talk—we have a lot of catching up to do." Spiritual writers prescribe coming into God's presence in this manner as the appropriate and normal way to begin all prayer.[1]

I have had to work at recognizing that I live in the Lord's presence. The notion that God resides in a place far distant from me lurks in my mind. Haven't we all at some time imagined space as an immense void, with God sequestered in his heaven at its farthest limits? We may even have pictured a human-like God with a few angels rattling around empty space, so remote that we presume he could not be bothered with us.[2] Perhaps more than anything else, such a mind-set blocks our receiving the gift of God's loving care and presence. When we entertain such views we feel isolated on our obscure planet. Thus we doom ourselves to seek a distant God who seems to be far beyond our reach. Nothing could be further from the truth.

Reflecting on God's presence has taught me that space is not devoid of God, and heaven is not far away. Or, stated more accurately, space is full of God, and heaven is everywhere.

We are not seeking a God who holes himself up in a far corner of the universe. We need only look around us because God is right at hand. He *is* everywhere, and therefore near us, for he permeates everything he created. "Your imperishable spirit," says Solomon, "is in all things" (Wis. 12:1 NAB). As St. Paul proclaimed to the Athenians, "Indeed he is not far

---

### God Fills All Space

God does not occupy space; yet we say, and say rightly, that God is everywhere. *Everywhere* is clearly a word of space: everywhere is the space occupied by everything. Therefore to say that God is everywhere is to say that God is in everything . . . God transcends all things; but He is immanent, in some way abiding in all things too . . . He is everywhere; that is, He is in all things, because the effect of His power is upon all things: "Do I not fill heaven and earth?" (Jeremiah 23:24).

The phrase "God is everywhere" means that God is in everything. Clearly a spiritual being is not in a material being as water is in a cup. We must look for a different meaning for the word "in." A spiritual being is said to be where it operates, in the things that receive the effects of its power. My soul, for instance, is *in* every part of my body, not by being spread out so that every bodily part has a little bit of soul to itself, but because the soul's life-giving energies pour into every part of the body. Everything whatsoever receives the energy of God, bringing it into existence and keeping it there; that is the sense in which God is omnipresent, is everywhere, in everything.

—Frank J. Sheed (1897–1981), *Theology and Sanity* and *Theology for Beginners*[3]

---

from each one of us. For 'In him we live and move and have our being'" (Acts 17:27–28). So today on my predawn walk I became aware of God's nearness in his handiwork: the full moon that shone his light on my path, the frogs that croaked his praises from the marsh, and the birds that began to sing thanks for the morning at first light.

**Heaven on Earth**

We may also hold mistaken notions about heaven. I think that art like the Sistine Chapel ceiling with angels and saints swirling about a long-bearded God, gorgeous as it is, has greatly contributed to our inadequate views. Don't we sometimes conceive of heaven as God's home above the sky? The place we go when we die if we've been good? Heaven is God's home and we will be abiding with him. But heaven is not a physical place, located perhaps on a planet at the edge of the universe. Heaven is God's living space and it exists wherever he is. In Scripture and Christian history the very word "heaven" speaks of God's presence.[4] For example, when Jacob dreamt of a ladder uniting heaven and earth and heard God's assurance of his presence, he exclaimed: "How awesome is this place! This is none other than the house of God, and this is the gate of heaven" (Gen. 28:17). Heaven surrounds us because God is in everything and is with us. When God touches our lives he acts not from a distant place above the sky. He reaches out to us from heaven—his living space with us, that is, his presence.

This morning I walked my usual two-mile route. I left my neighborhood, strode along an already busy thoroughfare, passed the local cemetery and then reversed my steps. I did not appear to passersby to be doing anything out of the ordinary—

just a man out for exercise. But I really was doing something extraordinary. I was walking in heaven because I was aware of God's presence everywhere around me.

## God Dwells in Us

God is present all around us, but he has also arranged to be present *in* us. "I will ask the Father," promised Jesus, "and he will give you another Advocate, to be with you forever. This is the Spirit of truth . . . You know him, because he abides with you, and he will be in you" (John 14:16–17). By his death and resurrection, Christ established a new relationship between God and us. He sealed our union with God by giving us the Holy Spirit. At our baptism, which is our sacramental participation in Jesus's death and resurrection (see Rom. 6:3–7), he sends the Spirit to dwell in us, immersing us in the divine presence. It happened for me as an infant. I was plunged into the Spirit on August 17, 1941, when my parents took me to St. Anne Church at Castle Shannon, Pennsylvania, and Fr. Angel (his real name) baptized me.

When we are baptized the Holy Spirit also makes God present to us by incorporating us into the body of Christ, the church. In this community we share Christ's own divine life with millions of Christians. The Holy Spirit animates the body of Christ. With his gifts and graces he draws God near to us and us near to God.

Especially when the community gathers for worship, the Spirit makes Christ present on our altars in the sacrament of the Eucharist. At Mass the celebrant invokes the Spirit, and a little bread and wine become the body and blood of Christ. Jesus said, "Anyone who eats this bread will live for ever; and the bread that I shall give is my flesh, for the life of the world . . . Whoever eats my flesh and drinks my blood lives in me and I live in that person" (John 6:51, 56 NJB). Thus Christ really comes to us in the Eucharist. When we receive the Eucharist, in a sacramental rather than a physical way, like Mary we become God-bearers, carrying in our hearts the Lord of the universe.

## Watching and Listening

God is always near, close enough to breathe his Spirit on us. He approaches us, but does not force himself on us. God waits patiently for us to notice him. It's up to us to spot the signs and discern the messages he sends. Becoming aware of God's presence is an art that we can learn only by honing our skills of watching and listening.

### Paying Attention to God

Long ago Jacopone di Todi (d. 1306), a great medieval Franciscan poet, said that we live as people locked in a castle, and that God wants to break through to us by appealing to our sight, hearing, . . . touch, and even smell. The more we become aware that God's love pursues us, the more we will experience the richness of the mercy he wants to show us. And as we let God touch our spirits through our senses, we will begin to practice the mysterious art called contemplation. Contemplation is nothing more than a constant awareness of the presence of God as we go about our daily lives.

. . . [T]oo often people are preoccupied with mastering techniques of contemplative prayer. We need to be occupied with listening to God and not simply listening to ourselves. Paying attention to God's voice is the essence of contemplation. He can speak to us through our desires and our inner experiences as well as through the world around us. God is calling us, and the basic technique of contemplation is to learn how to listen to him.

—Benedict Groeschel, CFR[5]

Brother Lawrence (ca. 1611–91), the renowned practitioner of the presence of God, says that he worked at mastering the art for ten years before it became a joyous habit free of troubles.[6] I take that as encouragement because I have a long way to go in developing my watching and listening skills. A recent decision to take morning walks has enhanced my ability to sense the Lord's presence in his creatures, as I reported above. My two-year-old grandson Max, who examines everything in his path with an aggressive curiosity, has been teaching me to be more observant of the heavenly things in my path.

I have been watching more for signs of God in my daily experiences. Not that all of my thoughts are on heavenly things—most are not, but the few that are draw me nearer to the Lord. For example, last Sunday Fr. Charlie Mitchell, our pastor, held up newly baptized baby Luke to the welcoming applause of the congregation. The thought occurred to me that no matter what big event CNN may report today, Luke's baptism was among the most important things that would happen anywhere in the world. The idea that by grace little Luke would now live eternally lifted my mind to God.

Recently God made his care known to me in a material way so demonstratively that I could not miss it. A mechanic told me that my beloved 1996 Ford Taurus was doomed and was not worth repairing. If I were to ask the guys at NPR's *Car Talk* how long it would last, they would ask me, "What time is it now?" As I pulled into the driveway wondering what to do, Margaret, my next-door neighbor, called out to me. She said that her son had bought her a new car and that she wanted to sell me her vintage and well-maintained Chrysler Concorde. She sold it to me for a steal the next day.

Paying attention to our experiences can help us become aware of God's presence. We can see his faithfulness in a long-time friend, his love in the couple who welcomes a recovering cancer patient into their home, his humility in the businessman in the Armani suit who helped us change a flat tire, his compassion in the family that volunteers at the homeless shelter, and his mercy in the woman who forgave the loan she made to an out-of-work single parent. I could go on, but you get the idea.

## Praying in God's Presence

We experience the benefits of practicing God's presence most when we take time to pray. If we are accustomed to living in God's presence, we can more easily enter into a conversation with him. But if we remain unaware of him, we may be talking to ourselves instead.

As I have already explained, attending to God's presence is the first activity of my prayer time. My undisciplined mind would rather busy me with planning my other activities, so I have developed some ways of staying focused on the Lord.

Sometimes I simply recall that I am opening my heart to God who is self-existent, independent, eternal, unchangeable, all powerful, all knowing, all loving, all just, all holy, and perfect. Or I might enter God's presence by reflecting on a Scripture text that draws me near to him. For instance, I recognize the Lord's closeness when I pray such verses as these from Psalm 116:

> Alleluia! I am filled with love when Yahweh listens
>      to the sound of my prayer,
> when he bends down to hear me, as I call . . .

My heart, be at peace once again,
  for Yahweh has treated you generously.
He has rescued me from death, my eyes from tears,
  and my feet from stumbling.
I shall pass my life in the presence of Yahweh,
  in the land of the living.
  — Psalm 116:1–2, 7–9 NJB

I have also discovered that reverently making the sign of the cross awakens me to God's presence. Invoking the names of the Father, Son, and Holy Spirit gives me access to them. These names that God revealed in Scripture are not mere labels. Calling on them brings me into contact with the persons of the Trinity. Sometimes I just let my body do the talking for me by humbling myself before God by bowing or kneeling.

So I let the Spirit lead me in choosing one or more of these ways of becoming aware of God's presence. And then I am ready to converse with him.

God has made it easy for us to live in his presence. Since he does not hide on a planet in a galaxy far, far away, we don't need to be spiritual astronauts to find him. He has arranged things so that he is always near. The Old Testament proclaims "God is with us" (Isa. 8:10). He appears to us everywhere in his creation. As Jeremiah reported, God declares his universal presence by asking, "Who can hide in secret places so that I cannot see them? . . . Do I not fill heaven and earth?" (Jer. 23:24). In the new creation the Father, Son, and Holy Spirit have come to be with us and in us. "I will not leave you orphaned; I am coming to you," Jesus said just before his death. "On that day you will know that I am in my Father, and you in me, and I in you" (John 14:18, 20). In his last words before he returned to his Father, Jesus promised to be with us always (see Matt. 28:20).

So the Lord surrounds us and fills us. He gently presses himself on us, wanting us to learn the art of living in his presence.

Think
- When have you been aware of God's presence?
- What experiences called your attention to God?
- How did these experiences of God affect you? What benefit did they bring you?
- Do you acknowledge God's presence when you pray?

Pray
Take fifteen minutes to pray. Consider these questions:

- Do you watch and listen for God's presence in your daily experiences?
- What steps might you take to learn how to become more aware of God's presence?

Act
- Select one of the steps you decided you might take to become more aware of God's presence.
- For the next two weeks apply this step daily.
- At the end of two weeks, assess your experience. Write down what you learned.
- Then select another step and repeat the process.

# 4

## Praying in the Spirit

I have learned to watch for the Holy Spirit's involvement in my life. The way Luke tells it in his Gospel, the Spirit keeps very busy moving in people's lives. He overshadowed Mary, he flooded Elizabeth with his presence, inspired Zechariah to prophesy about his son, guided Simeon to the infant Jesus, revealed the child to the prophetess Anna, and so on (see Luke 1:35, 41, 67; 2:26, 38). So I start every day by inviting him to take the lead in my prayer time.

I learned about the Holy Spirit as a boy. Sister Angelica, my first-grade teacher at St. Anne School in Castle Shannon, Pennsylvania, taught me that at my baptism the Holy Spirit had made me a child of God. Although it was eternally significant, at the time that fact made little difference to me. Then at age twelve, when I was in seventh grade, Sr. Johnnette prepared me for the sacrament of confirmation. She told me that the sacrament would make me a soldier of Christ. At the bishop's hand

I would receive the Holy Spirit and high-sounding gifts such as wisdom, piety, and fortitude.

On the day of the big event, I lined up in church with my friends—girls in white dresses and boys in blue suits with bright red ties. With fear and trembling I approached the bishop. He touched my forehead with oil, quickly wiped it off, and patted me on the cheek. That afternoon and the next day I kept trying to feel like a soldier of Christ. But since I did not experience any new strength nor recognize any gifts, my preteen brain decided that nothing had happened. I thought that if I couldn't feel the Spirit, he had not come to me. I concluded that somehow he had taken bad aim and missed me.

Of course I had received the Spirit in the sacrament, but I did not know how to relate to him or to exercise his gifts. I allowed him to remain dormant, because I had not learned to expect him to act in my life. But years later as a graduate student at the University of Notre Dame, I received the experience of the Spirit I had wanted as a kid. He came to me as a gift that transformed my life.

**Renewed in the Holy Spirit**

A little background will help me tell how the Holy Spirit renewed me. Shortly after I enrolled at Notre Dame in 1963, I connected with an informal community of students and faculty very much like Chi Rho. For a year I split my time between studying and doing what I believed was the Lord's work on the campus. In the spring of 1964 I married Mary Lou Cuddyre, my high school sweetheart, who shared my Christian commitment and experience. To my surprise, a year later I flunked my master's exam, a disastrous first for someone who

### Breaking the Verbal Barrier

Living water is spring water or river water that flows. Stagnant water has no outlets. For the Holy Spirit to be truly alive in us there must be outlets, and the Holy Spirit has provided them . . .

The first outlet gift is *praise*. The fire at Pentecost turned the befuddled community of the disciples into a blaze of praise. This praise did not consist in just reciting prayers or psalms of praise. It was so powerful that it broke the verbal barrier and gushed forth in tongues. That was the first sign that the Holy Spirit had truly come upon the community. So it is meant to be for us when we receive the Holy Spirit, who is the loving praise, the dance of the Father and the Son. We are moved to give our lips and our tongue over to the Holy Spirit so that his praise can flow through us. . . . Yielding to tongues may look and feel like going back to infancy. In fact, it is just the opposite. It is not going back before reason; it is going beyond it. It doesn't mean losing your mind and your ability to think . . . It is the heart talking to God beyond the limits of ordinary speech. St. Augustine called it a "jubilation."

—George T. Montague, SM, *Holy Spirit, Make Your Home in Me*[3]

had always been an A student. I raged at God because I thought he should have helped me—I thought I had been helping him. So I stopped praying and abandoned all my campus Christian activities. As a result I plunged into a severe depression. I made life miserable for Mary Lou (just ask her). But she and my friends kept praying for me and reaching out to me until I gradually emerged from my funk a year later. Although some depression lingered, I started to pray again and resumed my involvements with my colleagues.

Late that summer word buzzed among the groups at Duquesne and Notre Dame about an unusual book. The buzz was really about an experience called "baptism in the Holy Spirit" that David Wilkerson described in *The Cross and the Switchblade*.[1] That the Holy Spirit was working among twentieth-century Christians, just as he had among first-century Christians, fascinated me. I was intrigued that the Spirit was enabling a country pastor to rescue street kids in Manhattan.

Wilkerson explained that Scripture presented baptism in the Holy Spirit as a normal part of the Christian life. He made it clear that he was not discussing a theoretical theological truth. Rather he described a stunning experience of the Holy Spirit that turned lives upside-right, one that was available to all believers. He pointed to Jesus's promise that his disciples would "be baptized with the Holy Spirit" (Acts 1:5). And he referred readers to the realization of the promise at Pentecost when the disciples were "filled with the Holy Spirit and began to speak in other tongues" (Acts 2:4 RSV).

I found Wilkerson's reasoning persuasive. The evidence of Scripture and his testimony to the transforming power of the Spirit convinced me. I believed in the Holy Spirit. The possibility that I too might receive such a spiritual empowerment thrilled me. It seemed to be just what I needed.

Early in 1967 word reached Notre Dame that members of Chi Rho at Duquesne had been baptized in the Holy Spirit. Under the leadership of Dr. Storey and another professor, about twenty-five students had participated in a weekend retreat. The teachers told them to prepare by reading the Acts of the Apostles and to be open to the Spirit. Two of the students, Patti Gallagher (now Patti Mansfield) and David Mangan agreed that they would pray for a renewal of the gift of the Spirit they had received in the sacrament of confirmation. On Saturday evening something incalculable occurred. David entered the chapel and quickly found himself prostrate before the tabernacle, full of joy, and laughing. Patti entered the chapel a few hours later. She said a prayer of unconditional surrender to Jesus and also found herself prostrate as she was flooded with

### One Spirit, Many Gifts

*The water that I will give will become in them a spring of water, gushing up to eternal life (John 4:14).* This is a new kind of water, a living, leaping water, welling up for those who are worthy. But why did Christ call the grace of the Spirit water? Because all things are dependent on water; plants and animals have their origin in water. Water comes down from heaven as rain, and although it is always the same in itself, it produces many different effects, one in the palm tree, another in the vine, and so on throughout the whole of creation . . .

In the same way the Holy Spirit . . . apportions grace to each person as he wills. Like a dry tree that puts forth shoots when watered, the soul bears the fruit of holiness when repentance has made it worthy of receiving the Holy Spirit. Although the Spirit never changes, the effects of his action, by the will of God and in the name of Christ, are both many and marvelous.

The Spirit makes one person a teacher of divine truth, inspires another to prophesy, gives another the power of casting out devils, enables another to interpret holy Scripture. The Spirit strengthens one person's self- control, shows another how to help the poor, teaches another to fast and lead a life of asceticism . . . His action is different in different people, but the Spirit himself is always the same.

—St. Cyril of Jerusalem (ca. 315–86), *On the Holy Spirit*, a catechetical instruction in *The Office of Readings According to the Roman Rite*[4]

the love of God. About half of the students were also baptized in the Spirit during the weekend.[2]

On Saturday, March 4, Dr. Storey arrived at Notre Dame. At a prayer meeting that evening he shared about the events at Duquesne. "I no longer have to believe in Pentecost," he said. "I have seen it." The next evening he came to our apartment where nine men and women had gathered to hear more about baptism in the Spirit and maybe to receive it. Among them were my friends Kevin Ranaghan, a theology grad student, and his wife Dorothy, also a grad student, who had been a member of Chi Rho. After a long discussion and many questions, we asked Dr. Storey to pray for us. He asked us to kneel and invited the Lord to come among us. Then he laid hands on each of us, praying that Jesus would baptize us in the Holy Spirit.

The next day everyone shared that they had experienced the Spirit and testified to his working in them in new ways—everyone but me. I told Dr. Storey that I believed the Scripture about the outpouring of the Spirit, but felt that there must be an asterisk on the promise that said "except Bert Ghezzi." He advised me to wait and see what the Spirit would do. He assured me that something would happen soon.

As Dr. Storey predicted, within a few days I had evidence that I had been baptized in the Spirit. I sensed the residues of my depression lift. A new freedom was spreading throughout my being. Kevin Ranaghan laughed as he told me he felt like a toddler released from his playpen. I laughed as I said, "Me too."

### A Breakthrough in Prayer

During the week after we had been baptized in the Spirit, none of us received the gift of tongues. But since speaking in tongues seemed to be normal to the experience of the Spirit, we desired it. (However, I believe now as I did then, that a person can be baptized in the Spirit without yielding to the gift of tongues. I know many Spirit-filled Christians who have never prayed in an unlearned language.)

At Dr. Storey's suggestion, we sought the advice of Ray Bullard, a deacon at Calvary Temple, a Pentecostal church in South Bend. On Monday evening, March 13, Ray welcomed us at his home. He received us in a basement room that years before the Holy Spirit had directed him to finish in expectation of a special event. Ray believed that Notre Dame students seeking the gift of tongues was quite special, so he had invited eleven Pentecostal pastors and their wives to help him talk to us about it.

We spent several hours arguing politely with the ministers. They held the Pentecostal doctrinal opinion that we had not been baptized in the Spirit because we had not manifested "tongues as initial evidence." Dorothy and Kevin, our main spokespersons, represented our conviction that we had received the baptism of the Spirit and did not need to speak in tongues to prove it. But we assured our hosts of our desire to receive the gift. Neither side gave an inch, and by midnight the friendly disputation ended in a draw.

"Well," said one of the pastors, "do you want to speak in tongues or don't you?" We said that we did. Then the ministers laid hands on us and in a few moments we all began to pray in new, unlearned languages. I remember it as a solemn, but joyous event.

I went home on a spiritual high. I spent most of the early morning hours sitting in my rocking chair and praying in tongues. I was exhilarated, but not ecstatic, since I was in control, starting and stopping at will. As I exercised the gift, I sensed the Holy Spirit flowing through me and transforming the way I prayed. He was inspiring me to praise and adore the Lord, which I recognized as a brand new experience. Thanking God, repenting for sins, and interceding for others had always dominated my prayer. I did worship the Lord with psalms and Scripture, but never realized before that my adoring him had not been experiential. Praying in tongues was a breakthrough for me. The experience of praising God in an unlearned language revolutionized my prayer life. From the time of that wonderful evening at Ray Bullard's when I first prayed in tongues, I have sensed the Holy Spirit inspiring me to devote more of my prayer time to adoration. I still pray in tongues every day, but I now spend more time worshiping the Lord in my native tongue.

## Exercising Spiritual Gifts

Being baptized in the Spirit occasioned another breakthrough for me. It opened me to exercising gifts that I received in baptism and confirmation. In these sacraments the Holy Spirit confers gifts to strengthen us for Christian living. Four are workings of the Spirit that illumine our minds: wisdom, knowledge, understanding, and counsel. Three work in our hearts to bind us to the Lord: piety, reverence, and fortitude. I had received these gifts as a child, but never recognized them. When the Spirit renewed my life he activated them in me. He began to work through them in my daily life, and he still does. For example, he gives me insight into puzzling Scripture texts and practical wisdom for caring for my family. And he floods my heart with devotion that overflows into my daily prayer.

The Holy Spirit also gives every Christian gifts designed to build up the body of Christ (see 1 Cor. 12:4–11; Eph. 4:11–13). These spiritual gifts come in a great diversity and include charisms for leadership, teaching, and serving in the Christian community. "Each one of you has received a special grace," said St. Peter, "so, like good stewards . . . put it at the service of others" (1 Pet. 4:10 NJB). We should all expect the Spirit to confer such gifts on us and to show us how to use them for the good of others and to build up the church.

After I was baptized in the Spirit it became clear that the Lord was giving me a gift for communication. As a young man I recognized that I had a natural ability to explain things clearly. The Holy Spirit has shaped this skill into a gift that I can use in

### Opening to the Holy Spirit

Come, Creator Spirit, come
from your bright heavenly throne,
come take possession of our souls,
and make them all your own.

You who are called the Paraclete,
best gift of God above,
the living spring, the vital fire,
sweet christ'ning and true love.

You who are sev'nfold in your grace,
Finger of God's right hand,
his promise, teaching little ones
to speak and understand.

O guide our minds with your blest
    light,
with love our hearts inflame;

and with your strength, which ne'er
    decays,
confirm our mortal frame.

Far from us drive our deadly foe;
true peace unto us bring;
and through all perils lead us safe
beneath your sacred wing.

Through you may we the Father know,
through you th'eternal Son,
and you the Spirit of them both,
thrice-blessed Three in One.

All glory to the Father be,
with his co-equal Son;
the same to you, great Paraclete,
while endless ages run.

—Rabanus Maurus (776–856), *Veni, Creator Spiritus*[5]

his service. I describe it as a capacity to encourage others with words. I have learned to use it in one-on-one relationships, in giving talks, and in writing. I like to think that my exercising this gift helps to advance God's kingdom in some small way.

## Transformation in Christ

Being baptized in the Holy Spirit was also a breakthrough for me in my Christian growth. For instance, for years I had wanted to overcome bad habits that caused me to sin—my persistent anger and critical spirit, to name two. I had tried to say no to them with little success. But empowered by the Spirit I have been able to chip away at these evil inclinations somewhat more effectively.

As St. Paul says, the Spirit enables us to put to death our self-indulgent habits (see Rom. 8:13). He prompts us to replace them with good behaviors that make us more like Christ. Paul calls these character traits "fruit of the Spirit" (see Gal. 5:22–23). In my case the Holy Spirit daily gives me the grace to exchange my anger for patience and to trade my critical spirit for gentleness.

Baptism in the Spirit does not instantly eliminate our sinful tendencies and advance us to perfection in holiness. But to our great advantage it does enhance the Holy Spirit's work of transforming us in Christ (see 2 Cor. 3:18). Daily I open myself to this grace by praying one of the ancient canticles to the Holy Spirit that saints like Teresa of Avila testify promoted their Christian growth.

My experience with the Holy Spirit is not special. Nor is it unique. Being baptized in the Spirit is the biblical norm for all believers in Christ. It was so for the first Christians and it is still so for us today.

To get the picture check out the Acts of the Apostles: everyone who believed in Jesus received the Holy Spirit with manifestations that observers could see and hear (see Acts 2, 8, 10, and 19). Jesus himself described the release of the Spirit in believers as unmistakably experiential: "He cried out, 'Let anyone who is thirsty come to me, and let the one who believes in me drink. As the scripture has said, "Out of the believer's heart shall flow rivers of living water."' Now he said this about the Spirit . . ." (John 7:37).

Today millions of Christians have received the baptism in the Spirit and are exercising the spiritual gifts described in the New Testament. For example, 120 million Catholics worldwide have been baptized in the Spirit.[6] Like me they have enjoyed breakthroughs in their prayer, spiritual gifts, and in their Christian growth.

This renewal in the Spirit is available to you just for the asking. Jesus said: "Ask, and it will be given you . . . If you then, who are evil, know how to give good gifts to your children, how much more will the heavenly Father give the Holy Spirit to those who ask him!" (Luke 11:9, 11). The key, as I discovered, is expecting the Lord to act and fulfill his promises. You can count on him to do it. The Lord's offer is on the table.

Think
- Do you believe that you have received the Holy Spirit?
- In what ways have you experienced the action of the Holy Spirit?
- What gift or gifts has the Spirit given you for building up the church?
- In what areas of your life would you like the Holy Spirit to work?

Pray
Take fifteen minutes to pray. Consider the following:

- Are you open to asking the Lord to renew your life in the Spirit?
- Do you expect him to give you spiritual gifts?
- Do you have any obstacles to receiving a renewal in the Spirit? If so, what would it take to remove them?

Act

- Read the Acts of the Apostles 1:1–5 and 2:1–13.
- Read Luke 11:9–13.
- Ask the Lord to renew you in the Holy Spirit, giving you the experience of his presence and a breakthrough in your life of prayer.

# 5

## Praying with Thanksgiving

Prayers of thanksgiving make up a big part of all my daily prayer times. I thank the Lord for all the marvels of his creation and love. I praise him for this vast universe of one hundred billion galaxies, for this beautiful planet he made as a dwelling for us, his sons and daughters, and for the Word made flesh, who dwelt among us as Jesus Christ, in whom we have salvation and eternal life.

I also express my gratitude to God for a long list of his kindnesses to me. I thank him for creating me from nothing. For sustaining me in being. For giving me a human nature made in his own image. For conferring on me a share of his own divine life at my baptism. For my good mother, father, sisters, and brother. For my lovely wife, children, grandchildren, and a small army of friends. For always taking care of my needs. For removing the mountain of my sins as far as east is from

## Antidote for Dryness

Thanking also belongs to prayer. Thanking is a new, inward knowing, with great reverence and loving awe. It is a turning of our self with all our might to the working that our good Lord stirs us to, rejoicing and thanking Him inwardly. Sometimes because of its abundance, it [thanking] breaks out audibly and says, "Good Lord, many thanks! Blessed may you be!" Sometimes, when the heart feels nothing because it is dry or else because of the temptation of our enemy, it is driven by reason and by grace to cry out to our Lord, audibly going over His blessed passion and His great goodness. Then the virtue of our Lord's word turns into the soul, quickens the heart, by His grace starts it working properly, and makes it pray most blissfully. To rejoice truly in our Lord is a most blissful, lovely thanking in his sight.

—Julian of Norwich (ca. 1342–1423), *The Revelation of Divine Love in Sixteen Showings*[1]

west. And for extending to me the opportunity to share in the saving work of Christ.

On days when I feel like praying, giving thanks causes joy to well up and overflow in me. I feel as though I am participating in the thanksgiving songs that ring through Scripture, from the hymn of Moses at the exodus to the canticles of the saints in Revelation. But when dryness has set in and I don't feel much like praying, I lift my spirit by thanking the Lord for everything he has done. Julian of Norwich, the great anchoress and mystic, says that thanking Christ for his passion and goodness to us "quickens the heart, by his grace starts it working properly, and makes it pray most blissfully" (see sidebar). I experience this as the joy that Paul calls a fruit of the Spirit (see Gal. 5:22–23). Like all of these Spirit-inspired behaviors—for example love, patience, and self-control—joy is an activity, something that we do. I express my joy by giving thanks to the Lord, and it enlivens my prayer.

## Binding Me to God

When a friend gives us a gift or does something for us, we say "thank you." More than a mere polite gesture, expressing thanks tightens the bond that links us with our friend. It works the same way between the Lord and us. "What we see happening," says theologian Patrick D. Miller Jr., "in the human activity of beneficent act and grateful response identifies, if only indirectly and partially, what takes place in the relationship between God and human beings . . . that begins in the cry for help and moves from God's gracious response to the praise and thanksgiving it evokes."[2] This has been my experience. I sense a oneness with the Lord when I take time to give him thanks. Thanksgiving prayer makes me aware of my closeness to him, not so much as a feeling, but more as a recognition of its reality. It strengthens my bond of friendship with God.

## In All Circumstances

"Give thanks in all circumstances;" says St. Paul, "for this is the will of God in Christ Jesus for you" (1 Thess. 5:18). I apply this Scripture better in some circumstances than I do in others—in the good ones more easily than in the bad ones. I remember the exalted sense of thankfulness that I felt and expressed at the birth of each of my seven children. I recall, for example, how I was doused with gratitude as I drove home from the hospital celebrating the birth of a daughter. I am also grateful to the Lord for his many favors. For instance, once I prayed for his help when I was hopelessly lost in Washington, DC, and a parking-lot attendant gave me clear, easy-to-follow directions to my destination.

I have not always been thankful to the Lord when significant things have gone wrong. For example, I have responded ungratefully in the face of failures or rejection. I am correcting my behavior in such circumstances by considering the thankfulness of Jesus. I reflect on his prayers when he encountered rejection and anticipated his passion. When his opponents criticized him and towns where he had worked many miracles refused to believe, the Lord turned to his Father with a prayer of thanks: "I thank you, Father, Lord of heaven and earth, because you have hidden these things from the wise and the intelligent and have revealed them to infants; . . . for such was your gracious will" (Matt. 11:25). Before leaving for Gethsemane, while anticipating the worst circumstances of his life, Jesus still sang Psalms 113–18, the songs of thanksgiving for Passover.

I am confident that these meditations on Christ's prayers of thanks are preparing me to respond well to big things that go

---

**A Thanksgiving Song for Passover**

O give thanks to the Lord, for he is good;
    his steadfast love endures forever!
Out of my distress I called on the Lord;
    the Lord answered me and set me in a broad place.
With the Lord on my side I do not fear.
    What can mortals do to me?
Open to me the gates of righteousness, that I may enter through them
    and give thanks to the Lord.
I thank you that you have answered me
    and have become my salvation.
The stone that the builders rejected
    has become the chief cornerstone.

—Psalm 118: 1, 5–6, 19, 21–22

---

58

wrong. Mercifully, such events do not occur very often. I want to become like Paul and Silas, who sang songs of thanks through the night when they were jailed at Philippi (see Acts 16:25).

The little annoyances that occur many times every day frustrate me and expose one of my core faults. When something crosses me I respond with anger, not thanksgiving. If I step in dog feces while walking or spill coffee all over my desk, I react irritably. I am trying to change by applying the wisdom of St. Claude la Columbière (1641–82), a great Jesuit preacher of the seventeenth century:

> All our life is sown with tiny thorns that produce in our hearts a thousand involuntary movements of hatred, envy, fear, impatience, a thousand little fleeting disappointments, a thousand slight worries, a thousand disturbances that momentarily alter our peace of soul. For example, a word escapes that should not have been spoken. Or someone says something that offends us. A child inconveniences you. A bore stops you. You don't like the weather. Your work is not going according to plan. A piece of furniture is broken. A dress is torn.
>
> I know that these are not occasions for practicing very heroic virtue. But they would definitely be enough to acquire it if we really wished to.[3]

When I am able to thank the Lord for an inconvenience, I believe he chips away at my mountainous need to be in control. "Thanksgiving," says Patrick D. Miller Jr., "whether to other persons or God, is an inherent reminder that we are not autonomous or self-sufficient . . . Praise to God does that in a fundamental way as it directs our love away from self and *all* human sufficiency."[4] In my case it will take a lot more thanks and a lot more chipping away of my self-sufficiency before an adjective like "heroic" could even remotely apply to me.

## A Thanksgiving Sacrifice

Mary Lou and I attend our parish's contemporary Mass at 6 p.m. on Sundays, and I pray often at daily Mass. The heart of the Mass is a celebration of the Eucharist, a representation of Christ's once-for-all sacrifice that rescued us from sin and united us to God. The word "eucharist" derives from a Greek root that means "thanksgiving." At Mass I enjoy the privilege of participating in Christ's eternal sacrifice, offering myself with him in thanksgiving to the Father. I am expressing my gratitude for his giving me a share in his divine life through the death and resurrection of his Son.

The Mass takes its name from the Latin "*Ite, missa est.*" This is the charge to the congregation that concludes the liturgy, now translated as "The Mass is ended, go in peace to love and serve the Lord." I let my experience of worship at Mass flow into my daily prayer and life. It enhances my spirit of thanksgiving and strengthens me for my Christian service.

> **A Sacrifice of Thanksgiving**
>
> What shall I return to the LORD
> for all his bounty to me?
> I will lift up the cup of salvation
> and call on the name of the LORD,
> I will pay my vows to the LORD
> in the presence of all his
> people . . .
> I will offer to you a thanksgiving
> sacrifice
> and call on the name of the LORD.
> —Psalm 116:12–14, 17

Expressing gratitude to God gives shape and substance to my daily prayer. It fills me with joy, binds me to God, carries me through hardships, erodes my self-sufficiency, and engages me with Christ in his eternal self-giving. Those are big benefits for just saying thanks.

Think
- How often do you give thanks to God when you pray?
- What effect does thanksgiving prayer have on you? On your disposition for prayer? On your relationship with God?
- Paul says to give thanks in all circumstances. How have you tried to apply this instruction in your life?

Pray

Take fifteen minutes to pray and consider the following:

- What has God done for you that you should be thankful for?
- Make a list of everything he has done for you.
- What one thing could you do to train yourself to be thankful in all circumstances?

Act
- For the next two weeks, build thanksgiving into your daily prayer.
- After the second week, evaluate your experience. How did thanksgiving prayer affect you and your relationship with God?

# 6

## Praying with Scripture

Scripture shapes my morning prayer. Psalms weave through it, opening my heart to the Lord and evoking my responses to him. I read and reflect on longer passages that I study the night before with a commentary. These Scriptures present truths, events, or images that become themes for my prayer. I look for a few lines that activate my faith or apply to my life situation. As I meditate on these texts, I sense the Lord communicating to me. First thing in the morning I encounter him in his Word.

**Meeting God in the Bible**

My list of favorite authors includes Christian writers C. S. Lewis and F. J. Sheed and storytellers Rex Stout and Michael Connelly. They write superbly and engage me with their messages. I like them because they reveal something of themselves in their writing. In C. S. Lewis's works, for example, I meet an author who always looks at life from an eternal perspective. In Michael Connelly's books I encounter a novelist who has a passion for setting things right in the world. They put something of themselves in their books, but hidden behind their words they are not really present to me. I can say I "meet" Lewis and Connolly only metaphorically.

However, this is not the case with the Bible. The divine author reveals himself in the books of Scripture, and I meet him there not metaphorically, but actually. The church even draws a parallel between the Lord's real presence in the Eucharist and his presence in his Word. For example, the Second Vatican Council taught that "the Church has always venerated the divine Scriptures just as she venerates the body of the Lord,

> since, especially in the sacred liturgy, she unceasingly receives and offers to the faithful the bread of life from the table both of God's word and of Christ's body. She has always maintained them, and continues to do so, together with sacred tradition, as the supreme rule of faith, since, as inspired by God and committed once and for all to writing, they impart the word of God Himself without change, and make the voice of the Holy Spirit resound in the words of the prophets and Apostles. Therefore, like the Christian religion itself, all the preaching of the Church must be nourished and regulated by Sacred Scripture. For in the sacred books, the Father who is in heaven meets His children with great love and speaks with them; and the force and power in the word of God is so great that it stands as the support and energy of the Church, the strength of faith for her sons, the food of the soul, the pure and everlasting source of spiritual life. Consequently these words are perfectly applicable to Sacred Scripture: for "the word of God is living and active" (Heb.

4:12) and "is able to build you up and give you the inheritance among all who are sanctified" (Acts 20:32; see 1 Thess. 2:13).[1]

My first encounter with God in Scripture had a profound effect on my prayer and my life. My awakening to the Lord's presence in his word occurred at a Bible study sponsored by Chi Rho in the spring of 1961. I was aware of some Scripture from readings at Mass and from Bible history books we read in school. I had never studied Scripture or even read through a book of the Bible—not that any teacher had forbidden me to do it; reading Scripture was just not common practice among Catholics in the 1940s and 1950s.

Twenty or so students and faculty gathered as members of Chi Rho on Wednesdays at 3 p.m. to discuss the Gospel of John. We used the *New Testament Reading Guide* on John by Raymond E. Brown (1928–98). I still have my marked-up copy, now yellowed after half a century. At the time I did not know Fr. Brown, the renowned Scripture scholar, from Adam, so to speak, and I was just getting to know John. Honestly, I was lost most of the time on those Wednesdays, with the discussions rolling over my head.

One afternoon, however, Jesus stabbed me with these words: "If [anyone] loves me, he will keep my word, and my Father will love him, and we will come to him and make our home with him" (John 14:23 RSV).[2] I was stunned. I don't remember if I gasped for breath, but I might have. I was struck with the idea that God himself would make his home in me. That the one who created everything would relate to me so personally was news to me. Good news! You might have thought that a Catholic youth in his fourteenth year of Catholic education would have already grasped that notion. Somehow I hadn't.

On that Wednesday afternoon my mind wrapped around the truth of God's presence in me. I knew it as a fact, not as a sentiment. From that time the reality of John 14:23 has shaped my spirituality. Five decades later it still orients my life.

## God's Living Word

When I open my Bible at home, I handle it reverently. I acknowledge that I am coming into the Lord's presence. I remind myself that God who spoke the words on these pages thousands of years ago to people thousands of miles away will now speak also to me. I expect that what he says will have an effect on me. For the words of this author do not remain inert on the page like

### The Fruit of Scripture Study

The end or fruit of Holy Scripture is not something restricted, but the fullness of eternal happiness. These writings which contain "the message of eternal life" (John 6:69) were written, not only that we might believe in, but also that we might possess that everlasting life in which we shall see, and love, and be fulfilled of all we desire. Then we shall really know that "love of Christ that surpasses knowledge," and thus "be filled with all the fullness of God" (Eph. 3:19). This is the fullness to which the divine Scriptures would lead us, as is truly said in the words of the Apostle quoted above. Such, then, must be our goal and our intent in studying and in teaching the Scriptures, and also in hearing them.

And that we attain this fruit and end rightly, by the straight road of Scripture itself, we must begin at the beginning. That is, we must reach out in a spirit of pure faith to the Father of all light, and kneeling in our hearts, ask him to give us, through his Son and in the Holy Spirit, the true knowledge of Jesus Christ, and together with knowledge, love for him. By knowing and loving Christ, by being confirmed in faith and "grounded in love" (Eph. 3:17), we can know the breadth, length, and depth of Scripture, and, through such knowledge, attain unto the all-surpassing knowledge and measureless love which is the Blessed Trinity.

—St. Bonaventure (ca. 1218–74), *Breviloquium Prologue*[3]

those of mere human writers. God has assured us that the words he speaks will do his will in us. He promised that just as rain brings forth grain that produces bread for our tables, "so shall my word be that goes out from my mouth; it shall not return to me empty, but it shall accomplish that which I purpose, and succeed in the thing for which I sent it" (Isa. 55:11).

The writer of Hebrews says that the things that God intends to accomplish in us are matters of the heart: "Indeed, the word of God is living and active, sharper than any two-edged sword, piercing until it divides soul from spirit, joints from marrow; it is able to judge the thoughts and intentions of the heart" (Heb. 4:12). Sometimes the Lord just taps my heart with his two-edged sword, speaking a word of gentle correction or encouragement. At other times he pierces my heart with an insight into his truth or a conviction of my sin. So as I read Scripture the Lord gives me what I need most: the wisdom to choose to do what he wants me to. He speaks words intended to make me holy, and I want him to succeed. I feel as though I am a distant beneficiary of St. Paul's intercession for his beloved disciples. He always prayed that they would have the knowledge of God's will so that they would lead lives pleasing to him and bear good fruit (see Eph. 1:15–19; Phil. 1:9–11; Col. 1:9–12).

## Praying with Scripture

Eating meals and studying Scripture have a lot in common. Eating is essential for life. If we stop eating, we will grow weak and eventually stop living. The food we eat provides the nourishment our bodies require. We eat at regular times, and if we miss a meal we make it up. We should be approaching Scripture study in the same way.

Studying the Bible is essential for Christian living. Just as food nourishes our bodies, the Word of God nourishes our souls. Jesus himself said that "one does not live by bread alone, but by every word that comes from the mouth of God" (Matt. 4:4). If we don't reflect on Scripture we are starving our spiritual lives and putting ourselves at grave risk. Like taking regular meals, we must build Bible study into our schedule. Saints and scholars commonly recommend fifteen minutes with Scripture every day. Because getting into a routine assures perseverance, they also urge reading the Bible at a set time and place.

That's what I do. I devote about a quarter hour of my morning prayer time to Scripture. I usually read through a book of the Bible each month. I ask the Holy Spirit to guide me to a book and then I select one that appeals to me, trusting that the Spirit is prompting me. Sometimes I choose a book that the church is reading at Mass or the liturgy of the hours. I might pick a book that I studied years ago or one of my favorites, such as the Gospel of John, which I read once a year. Over the past year, in addition to John I have reflected on the first five books of the Bible, Proverbs, the Gospel of Matthew, and the Letters of Paul.

Over the years I have adopted an ancient method of prayerful Bible study called *lectio divina*, literally "divine reading," but commonly translated as "spiritual reading." *Lectio divina* developed as a way of praying with Scripture among men and women in monasteries, convents, and religious communities. But in recent years thousands of Catholic laypeople have adapted it and made it workable for them in their secular environments.[4] *Lectio divina* involves a series of overlapping and interchangeable movements. It includes reading a text of Scripture, meditating on it, praying with it, and applying it to life.

68

One of my earliest experiences with this way of study occurred when I was reading Romans, and I will refer to it as I explain the movements of *lectio divina*.

> Do you not know that all of us who have been baptized into Christ Jesus were baptized into his death? Therefore we have been buried with him by baptism into death, so that, just as Christ was raised from the dead by the glory of the Father, so we too might walk in newness of life.
>
> For if we have been united with him in a death like his, we will certainly be united with him in a resurrection like his. We know that our old self was crucified with him so that the body of sin might be destroyed, and we might no longer be enslaved to sin. For whoever has died is freed from sin. But if we have died with Christ, we believe that we will also live with him. We know that Christ, being raised from the dead, will never die again; death no longer has dominion over him. The death he died, he died to sin, once for all; but the life he lives, he lives to God. So you also must consider yourselves dead to sin and alive to God in Christ Jesus.
>
> —Romans 6:3–11

### Reading

The first activity of *lectio divina* is simply reading the text. Following the classic Catholic approach, we first attempt to understand what the human author was trying to say to his readers. We may need to consult a commentary to help us grasp the meaning of the passage. As I read Romans 6, I determined that Paul was reminding the Christians at Rome of the significance of their baptism. It was no mere cleansing, but a life-changing experience, as they had died to their old selves and risen to a new life in Christ. A commentary suggested to me that Paul may have had in mind the early Christian practice of baptism by immersion in a pool dramatizing the catechumen's death as a drowning—a burial in water—and his rising from the watery grave to a new life in Christ.

Having explored the original author's intent, then we must ask what the Lord may be saying to us. God was communicating a living word to the human author's community; now he wants to communicate a living word to us. My reading of Romans 6 deepened my appreciation of a truth I had not fully grasped. I believed the Lord wanted me to know that in some mysterious, sacramental way I had been crucified with him and had arisen with him from the tomb to a new life. I might even dare to say that "Christ died on the cross, and I died with him; and Christ rose from the tomb, and I rose with him." That insight was a spiritual eye-opener for me.

### Meditation

After a careful reading of the text, the next movement of *lectio divina* is meditation, which we may approach in a variety of ways. When reading a narrative like one of the Gospels we can imagine ourselves in the scene or in the person of one of the characters in the story. We might take a more analytical approach by focusing on a word or phrase that especially strikes us. Or we might reflect on an entire passage. Some of this reflection may have already begun as we tried to figure out what the Lord is saying to us through the Scripture.

For example, I had already reflected on the meaning of my baptism while seeking God's Word to me in Romans 6. Then as I meditated on the text, an event from the life of Chinese evangelist Watchman Nee (1903–73) came to mind. While reading Romans 6 in his second floor office he had a profound and startling realization of his death in Christ. He ran downstairs, grabbed a friend, and shouted, "Brother, do you know that I have died?"[5] The man must have thought that Nee was insane. As I reflected on him and the text, I knew that he was sane because he was truly in touch with reality. His dramatic announcement made me want to declare that I too had died in Christ to my old sinful self.

### Prayer

A third activity of *lectio divina* is praying with Scripture. We take the words of the text we have read along with our understandings and reflections and use them in a conversation with the Lord. We may take some time in silence, listening for God to say something in our thoughts about the Scripture. Then we may speak to him about what we have heard and understood of his Word to us. For example, when I read Romans 6 I find myself thanking the Lord for my baptism. I express my gratitude for his hideous and painful crucifixion that he allowed me to share sacramentally, letting me die with him without enduring his suffering. I thank him for his marvelous resurrection, that in his great mercy he allowed me to share and gain eternal life, even though because of my sin I deserved eternal death.

### Application

*Lectio divina*'s final movement is application. After reading, meditating, and praying with a Scripture, we look for ways to apply it to our life. I like to ask myself if there is any important thing I could do, and easily implement, to change my life in response to the text. Ease of implementation is crucial because I would soon abandon things that I found difficult. But important because my response should make a noticeable difference in my life. For instance, my reading of Romans 6 suggested a very practical way of dealing with temptation. I realized that having died with Christ I was dead to sin. So I decided to hold myself to that fact. When my besetting sins tempt me, I can say, "You can't get to me anymore because I'm dead to you. And dead men don't sin."

*Lectio divina* is not an arcane formula for praying with Scripture. Its movements—reading, meditating, praying, and applying—are not complicated. I was already using them in scriptural prayer before I knew their names. If you have been reading Scripture, you probably have done the same. If you haven't been reading the Bible, you should try this ancient approach.

### Constant Prayer

Saint Paul wraps up his first letter to the Thessalonians with a command that has puzzled Christians for centuries: "Rejoice always, pray without ceasing, give thanks in all circumstances; for this is the will of God in Christ Jesus for you" (1 Thess. 5:16–18). Being joyful, prayerful, and thankful sometimes, if not mostly, seems realistic. It's the "always" that baffles us. We may even learn how to embrace whatever comes with joy and gratitude. That's a matter of responding to grace and getting things in the right perspective. But praying without ceasing—that's another matter altogether.

### Praying Constantly

In order to keep God always in mind you should frequently pray this verse: "O God come to my assistance, O Lord make haste to help me" (see Ps. 70:1). With good reason this text has been selected from all of Scripture as a method of continual prayer. It encompasses all the emotions that human beings can experience. We can effectively apply it to any circumstance and use it to resist every temptation. Since the verse appeals to God against all danger, it expresses our humble dependence on him, our anxieties and fears, our admission of our own weakness, and our confidence in answered prayer. And it conveys the assurance of God's present and ever ready help. A person constantly calling on his protector can be sure that he is near . . .

So we will find this verse useful in all circumstances, whether adverse or prosperous and happy, because it confesses our absolute dependence on God: When a headache or drowsiness interferes with my spiritual reading, I must say, "O God come to my assistance, O Lord make haste to help me." . . . When I am struggling against a sexual temptation and a pleasant feeling draws me to say yes to it, I must cry out, "O God come to my assistance, O Lord make haste to help me." When anger or envy threatens to disturb my peacefulness and embitter me, I must force myself to pray, groaning, "O God come to my assistance, O Lord make haste to help me." . . .

. . . When dryness keeps me earthbound and blocks all spiritual thoughts, I can get free from this state of mind only by pleading, "O God come to my assistance, O Lord make haste to help me." When the Holy Spirit strengthens my soul, fills me with unspeakable joy, and enlightens my mind with new insights, in order to continue enjoying these graces I must pray, "O God come to my assistance, O Lord make haste to help me." . . .

This thought may be a saving formula for you, not only protecting you from all the devil's attacks, but also purifying you from your faults and sins, and leading you to that heavenly contemplation and that ineffable glow of prayer, which so few experience.

—*Conferences of John Cassian* (ca. 360–433)[7]

Paul did not make constant prayer a casual request. He directed it on God's authority. And he was addressing ordinary Christians like you and me, not Christians who exclusively devoted themselves to a life of prayer. So how do men and women immersed in the daily requirements of family life, work, childcare, service, and everything else manage to pray without ceasing?

St. Augustine (354–430) offered an answer that I find helpful. He says that we can make our desire for eternal life into a constant prayer: "When the Apostle tells us: *Pray without ceasing,* he means this: Desire unceasingly that life of happiness which is nothing if not eternal, and ask it of him who alone is able to give it."[6]

We stir our faith, hope, and desire for eternal life at our regular times of prayer and reflection on Scripture. We can learn to pray constantly by letting that desire spill over into our awareness throughout the day. Augustine recommends that we exercise our desire for God's gift by offering frequent, short prayers "hurled like swift javelins."[8] Praying with Scripture can assist us in this effort. During our prayer time and Scripture study, we should focus on a verse that seems to speak to us. We should dwell on it, turning it over in our mind, and fix it in our memory so that we can return to it during the day. We can repeat the verse often, hurling it heavenward, like a swift javelin.

For example, many years ago I stumbled on St. John Cassian's advice to pray at all times: "O God come to my assistance, O Lord make haste to help me." I still fire that verse off frequently. Currently, I find myself praying a line from Psalm 16 that touched my heart a few weeks ago: "You will teach me the path of life, unbounded joy in your presence, at your right hand delight for ever" (Ps. 16:11 NJB).

Repeating that verse gives me an assurance that he will guide me on the road to true happiness. Of course, I must listen to him and follow his directions. Otherwise I would be like Yogi Berra, who once said, "We're making good progress, but we're lost."

Think

- What is your experience of reading the Bible? Do you read Scripture occasionally? Regularly? Daily?
- Do you have a set time and place for reading the Bible?
- Do you believe that God speaks to you in Scripture?
- What text or texts of Scripture have spoken to you or touched you heart?

Pray

Take fifteen minutes to pray and consider the following:

- Are there any obstacles to your reading Scripture daily? What would it take to remove them?
- What would you have to change to build Scripture study into your daily routine?
- If you are reading Scripture daily, consider what you might do to enhance your approach to Bible study.

Act

- If you are not already reading Scripture daily, decide to study the Gospel of Mark for fifteen minutes every day for the next month. At the end of the month evaluate your experience and consider continuing to read Scripture daily.
- If you are reading the Bible daily, for the next month implement the enhancements that came to mind during your time of prayer.
- At the end of the month, consider your experience and renew your decisions about daily Scripture study.

# 7

## Listening to God

My wife and children tell me that I am not a good listener. I am afraid that's true. I often have to ask Mary Lou to repeat something she has said either because I was not paying attention or was distracted by something I was doing. It's also true that I have not always been a good listener to God. To open my spiritual ears over the years I disciplined myself to take a time of silence during my morning prayer. I also trained myself to listen for his voice and leadings throughout the day. I wanted to give the Lord opportunities to get through to me. I discovered that the more I listen to him, the more I hear. No surprise there!

### Hearing from God

Saint Paul's letter to the Ephesians is one of my favorite stopping places in the New Testament. I return to it frequently, and each time I discover something I had not noticed before. That testifies to the richness of God's revelation in Scripture, which brims over with fresh words that speak to our present circumstances.

Recently a verse in Ephesians struck me as I realized a deeper level of its significance. "Thus," wrote Paul, "he chose us in Christ before the world was made to be holy and faultless before him in love, marking us out for himself beforehand, to be adopted sons, through Jesus Christ" (Eph. 1:4–5 NJB). Even before God spoke the word that launched the universe, he had already planned to create us and bring us into the divine community. He wanted a family of children, men and women that could share his love. God desired to draw us into a relationship with him. He intended to bless us, to hold us close, and to care for us.

Whether we are aware of it or not, we live in God's presence.[1] Because he loves us without limit or conditions, he stays with us no matter what we do or where we go. God wants to tell us of his love and reveal his truths and his plans for our lives. He speaks to us in countless ways. We can hear God in our thoughts and desires, in Scripture and the liturgy, in our prayers and meditations, in conversations with friends and chance encounters with strangers, in affirmations and corrections, in books and art, in successes and failures, in the example and testimony of others, and in all of our daily experiences.[2]

On rare occasions God has spoken audibly to someone. For instance, once the Lord spoke to St. Francis of Assisi (1181–1226) from a crucifix, telling him to rebuild the church. But most often he communicates to us in our thoughts. Listening to God is the art of hearing in our mind what he is saying, and then responding to it. The more we work at it, the more skilled we will become at receiving his words. We will make some mistakes along the way. When we do we will be in good company. St. Francis, for example, thought that the

---

**The Value of Interior Silence**

The activity of the Spirit within us becomes more and more important as we progress in the life of interior prayer. It is true that our own efforts remain necessary . . . But more and more our own efforts attain a new orientation: instead of being directed toward ends we have chosen ourselves, instead of being measured by the profit and pleasure we judge they will produce, they are more and more directed to an obedient and cooperative submission to grace, which implies first of all an increasingly attentive and receptive attitude toward the hidden action of the Holy Spirit. It is precisely the function of meditation . . . to bring us to this attitude of awareness and receptivity. It also gives us strength and hope, along with a deep awareness of the value of interior silence in which the mystery of God is made clear to us.

—Thomas Merton (1915–68), *Contemplative Prayer*[3]

---

Lord wanted him to repair the dilapidated chapel where he was praying.[4] Later he figured out that God was calling him to renew the church by reviving the faith of its members. If we misunderstand an inspired thought at first, we can expect the Holy Spirit to correct our thinking.

## Are We Really Hearing God?

How can we tell that something we hear is really God speaking to us? We can use the ways that he has provided to test our listening. The Lord does not contradict himself. Nothing that we hear from him will conflict with Scripture or the teaching of the church. Recently, for example, on subsequent occasions at prayer I heard God tell me that he loved me, that he wanted to trade my hard heart for a new, soft one, and that he wanted me to embrace the role of writing and teaching he had for me in the body of Christ. I recognized each of these as authentic both because they conformed to Scripture and Catholic teaching and because I needed to hear them. The Lord's affirming his love for me delighted me. I welcomed his offer to transform my heart because I tend to be hard and hasty in judgments, and I want to change. And accepting my limited calling to write and occasionally teach prevents me from extending myself in activities beyond my scope. My listening to these words is bringing me great benefits.

Sometimes we receive an inner conviction that an insight comes from God. This is another test for our listening. When I once asked a Pentecostal minister how he knew God was speaking to him, he said, "I know it with my knower." As it happened for the pastor, sometimes the Holy Spirit also assures us within that a thought comes directly from God. We know it with our knower. We say, "Aha!" and celebrate the revelation.

I have enjoyed a number of "aha" experiences, some of which have changed my life significantly. Two of them occurred in 1975 when Mary Lou and I had five children, ranging in age from two to thirteen. That year I plunged into writing my first book, *Build with the Lord*. I was very excited about becoming an author and I thought I had something important to say. I was working more than forty hours a week, so I devoted all my spare time to writing. One morning at prayer the Lord gave me a wake-up call. He said, "You are paying more attention to this book than you are to your family. The book will last ten years and your children will last forever." I responded with decisive actions. I began spending one-on-one time with each of the older children. I also instituted the "snack," a time every night the family gathered in the kitchen for light food and conversation. I was taking steps in the right direction and pursued them for years. Here's the clincher that confirmed that I had heard from God—in 1985, exactly ten years after I had written *Build with the Lord*, the publisher notified me that the book was out of print!

Later in 1975 the Lord spoke to me through C. S. Lewis's essay, "The Weight of Glory." One night, after everyone had gone to bed, I stayed up reading and came across this stunning paragraph:

> It is a serious thing to live in a society of possible gods and goddesses, to remember that the dullest and most uninteresting person you talk to may one day be a creature which, if you saw it now, you would be strongly tempted to worship, or else a horror and a corruption such as you now meet, if at all, only in a nightmare. All day long we are, in some degree, helping each other to one or other of these destinies. It is in the light of these overwhelming possibilities . . . that we should conduct all our dealings with one another, all friend-ships, all loves, all play, all politics. There are no ordinary people. You have never talked to a mere mortal. Nations, cultures, arts, civilizations—these are mortal, and their life is to ours as the life of a gnat. But it is immortals whom we joke with, work with, marry, snub, and exploit—immortal horrors or everlasting splendors.[5]

I realized immediately that these words would change forever the way I viewed and treated my family. Deeply moved, I went room by room and looked at my sleeping wife and children, whom God created to have eternal life—my potential gods and goddesses, to use Lewis's image. I prayed for each of them. I resolved that I would strive to relate to each in ways that would move them toward their becoming eternal splendors. Have I succeeded in the effort? As you might guess, not always. But

81

when I do something that may move one of them in the wrong direction, I quickly repent and take corrective action.

## Bumping into God

God does not restrict his talking to us to our reflective moments at prayer. He takes any opportunity we may give him to communicate with us. Sometimes, for example, I have encountered him in acts of kindness. Recently, while I was recovering from surgery for several months, without my asking a neighbor moved our trash containers to the street for refuse pickup every week; a friend chauffeured me on errands and to events at church; a business associate of my daughter lent me

---

### Speak Lord, Your Servant Is Listening

Our Lord Jesus Christ will come to you and will show you his consolations, if you will make ready for him a dwelling place within. All that he desires in you is within yourself, and there it is his pleasure to be. There are between almighty God and a devout soul many spiritual visitings, sweet inward conversations, great gifts of grace, many consolations, much heavenly peace, and wondrous familiarity of the blessed presence of God . . .

"Speak Lord, for I your servant, am ready to hear you. I am your servant: give me wisdom and understanding to know your commandments. Bow my heart to follow your holy teachings, that they may sink into my soul like dew into the grass." . . .

"My son," says our Lord, "hear my words and follow them, for they are most sweet, far surpassing the wisdom and learning of all philosophers and all the wise men of the world. My words are spiritual and cannot be comprehended fully by man's intelligence. Neither are they to be adapted or applied according to the vain pleasure of the hearer, but are to be heard in silence, with great humility and reverence, with great inward affection of the heart and in great rest and quiet of body and soul."

—Thomas à Kempis (ca. 1380–1471), *The Imitation of Christ*[6]

---

a hospital bed; and another friend came regularly to pray for me. In all of these kindnesses I sensed God's tender care for me.

I have also heard the Lord speak to me in conversations. For example, although I love praying the psalms I have always had a difficulty with their expressions of hatred for enemies, both God's and mine. I wondered how I was to understand verses like "Do I not hate those who hate you?" or "In your faithful love annihilate my enemies" (Pss. 139:21; 143:12 NJB). One day I told Dr. Storey that I was uncomfortable praying such texts. He suggested that instead of taking the verses literally, I should interpret them as speaking of my sins, which were truly enemies. I think the Holy Spirit was giving me a gift through him. Now I use the "hate the enemies" psalms as prayers of repentance. I name some of my worst habits and pray, "Lord 'rescue me from my enemies . . . since in you I find protection . . . In your faithful love annihilate [my sins], destroy all those who oppress me, for I am your servant'" (Ps. 143: 9, 12 NJB).

A conversation with my friend Kevin Perrotta was also an eye-opener. Once at a party I told him that I had just read a book about sacraments by a well-known Catholic author. "He denies the church's teaching on baptism," I said; "says it just acknowledges our faith and has no power to change us."

"Oh, no!" exclaimed Kevin. "How about a power as great as creation!" I believe the Lord spoke to me in that retort. As I reflected on it, the Holy Spirit convinced me that the transformation God worked in baptism by putting us in Christ—elevating our human nature to a share in the divine nature—was on a par with the creative effort he had expended in the big bang. I realized that baptism's re-creation of one human being as a divinized person paralleled the original creation of the universe. As St. Paul says, "If anyone is in Christ, there is a new creation:

83

everything old has passed away; see, everything has become new!" (2 Cor. 5:17).

In other conversations God has spoken words of correction through friends that have led me to change my life. Once when I was having a difficult time with a teenage son, a friend called me aside and gave me his perspective on the situation. He said that I was holding my son to too high a standard of behavior. He advised me to back off in areas such as dress, orderliness, and achievement and only maintain a high expectation in morality. The Lord was making me aware that actually my son was having a difficult time with an overly demanding dad. I relaxed my standards, headed off the crisis predicted by my friend, and repaired the endangered relationship with my son. We have related well ever since.

Experiences such as these have alerted me to pay attention even to casual conversations with friends—God may be breaking through to me at any moment.

## Life Direction

In a little over four decades I have switched jobs seven times. After one big change from seven years of college teaching to magazine and book editing, I have worked for over thirty-five years for a series of publishing companies. I prayed long and hard daily before making these changes. I believe the Lord guided me through them with directions he gave me at prayer.

One day in February 1974, during my morning prayer time, I heard the Lord say that he wanted me to move to Ann Arbor, Michigan, where I would become editor of *New Covenant* magazine. This thought did not come to me in clearly worked-out sentences. Rather, I articulated it as an expression of a burning desire that formed in my consciousness. At the time I was living in Grand Haven, Michigan, and teaching history at Grand Valley State College. I was also serving as a leader in the fast-growing Catholic charismatic renewal movement. Only a few years old, *New Covenant* had become a chief means of communication that was generating the movement.

Because I really would have loved to edit the magazine, I figured I was hearing myself and not God. "Lord," I prayed, "I am not going to tell anyone that I heard this. If you want me to become editor of *New Covenant*, you will have to confirm it through someone else." I set his leading to one side, remembering it only occasionally at prayer, and went about teaching college freshmen about Western civilization.

A month later a letter arrived from Steve Clark, a leader of the Charismatic Renewal at Ann Arbor. He said that he and Ralph Martin, the founding editor of the magazine, thought that I should consider moving to Ann Arbor, where I would become editor of *New Covenant*, if it worked out for my family. Over the next six months, after much prayer and consideration, Mary Lou and I decided to make the move in October. Just before we drove away from Grand Haven, I sensed the Lord leading me to confirm our move with a Scripture text. I did something I rarely do. I opened the Bible randomly and my eyes fell on 2 Corinthians 3:5–6, which reads, "Our competence is from God, who has made us competent to be ministers of a new covenant." I felt a little thrill to realize that I had heard the Lord, listened to him, and did what he directed.

I have shared a few standout occasions when I have heard the Lord. But most of the time I still have to strain to listen to his gentle voice. I do not regard myself as an expert at listening to God. I have never developed a method for hearing him.

"The Lord is not a divine vending machine," says a friend, who cautions against taking a procedural approach to listening. I just try to pay attention to God, especially when I am praying. I have always struggled to quiet myself and listen for his word. I have learned to reserve moments of silence during my prayer times to let God have an opportunity to say something. Better pray-ers than I recommend that at the very least we take five minutes to listen during prayer.

And as much as possible I make myself aware of God's presence during the day, hoping to hear him in my experiences and in the people I encounter.

Think
- Do you take time at prayer to listen to God?
- Do you make yourself aware of his presence during the day?
- What have you heard the Lord say recently? What was the occasion of his speaking to you? Silence during prayer time? Reflecting on Scripture? A conversation? An experience? Other?

Pray
Take fifteen minutes to pray and consider the following:

- Do you give God your full attention when you pray?
- Does the way you pray make it difficult for you to listen?
- Do you need to rearrange your prayer time or increase it so that you can listen to God?
- What could you do to listen to God more effectively?

Act

- Select one action that occurred to you when you prayed. Pick one that is easy to implement, but which will enhance your listening to God.
- Decide to make the change and do it for a month. At the end of the month evaluate your experience. Make any adjustment you think necessary and continue the practice.

# 8

Relying on God

My dad died when I was twelve years old, and as a teen I subconsciously set out on a "father hunt." As I reported in a previous chapter, at eighteen I became a friend of Professor William Storey, who showed a real concern for me. Without my realizing it at the time, he became a spiritual father to me. Among his many gracious acts on my behalf, he taught me how to pray and live a dedicated Christian life.

Years later when I took stock of my "father hunt," I discovered that I had quietly entered a close relationship with my true father, God himself. The realization struck me as I meditated on what it had meant for me to live in the Spirit. The Holy Spirit had arranged for me to become the Father's adopted son. I had received the promise that St. Paul reported to the Ephesians: God "destined us for adoption as his children through Jesus Christ" (Eph. 1:5). What a wonderful gift it was to recognize that the Father loved me and wanted me as his child!

I enjoy this father–son relationship with God. I thank him for it in my daily prayer and I find myself trusting him a little more all the time. I don't feel that as his son I am entitled to special graces or supernatural interventions. But I am not afraid or shy about asking God for something that I need. To paraphrase St. Paul: as best I can I don't worry about anything, but in everything by prayer and supplication with thanksgiving, I make my requests known to God (see Phil. 4:5). I believe God always answers such prayers. Sometimes he says, "Yes, here is what you requested." Other times he may point to something better he has in mind for me. Even when he seems not to respond, I have found perspectives that help me deal with his silence. More about that later in this chapter.

**Answered Prayers**

I have grown in confidence to ask the Father for big things because he has granted my much needed smaller requests. The gospels have taught me to expect him to give me good things when I ask. Often in these cases he delivers the good thing at the last minute. I think he makes me wait on edge so that he can expand my trust in him to the maximum. Let me tell about two incidents of such answered prayer.

*The Lost Key*

Nearly two decades ago Mary Lou was hired to work at the circulation desk of The Winter Park Public Library. At the end of her first week she had lost her key to the library. This was no small matter. In the wrong hands the key could open the door for the theft of hundreds of valuable books, audios, and videos. Re-keying the library would cost hundreds of dollars

### The Father's Generosity

Ask, and it will be given you; search, and you will find; knock, and the door will be opened for you. For everyone who asks receives, and everyone who searches finds, and for everyone who knocks, the door will be opened. Is there anyone among you who, if your child asks for bread, will give a stone? Or if the child asks for a fish, will give a snake? If you then, who are evil, know how to give good gifts to your children, how much more will your Father in heaven give good things to those who ask him!

—Matthew 7:7–11

and may have cost Mary Lou her job. So we prayed intently for the Lord to help us find the key. We even used my mother's handy prayer that always seemed to work: "Jesus, lost and found, help us to find what we've lost."

We searched everywhere. We dumped Mary Lou's purses and briefcases. We scoured the van and the car. We raked through the lawn near the driveway. We ransacked the house. No sign of the key.

On Monday morning of her second week at work, Mary Lou decided with fear and trembling that she would have to report the lost key to her supervisor. "This cannot happen, Lord," I prayed. "Let me find that key now." At that moment I felt God was directing me to check the van one more time. Since we had searched there many times, doing so again did not seem promising. But when I looked under the driver's seat, the key was right there in plain sight!

How had that happened? Had we simply not seen it before? Had some child played a silly prank, wised up, and put it where we would find it? (You know, one of those things an adult child will laughingly reminisce about at Thanksgiving dinner: "Remember the time we hid Mother's library key?") Or did the Lord find it and put it there because he loved Mary Lou?

No matter how the key ended up under the driver's seat, we thanked the Lord for a little miraculous answer to our prayer.

### Breakfast with the Pope

In January 1995 I was working as the editorial director for Servant Publications. That month we sold a remarkable ten thousand copies of a devotional by Pope John Paul II. At a meeting I told the publishing team that we should immediately bring out another book by the pope that would piggyback on the success. Remembering William G. Ward, a nineteenth-century writer who wished for a papal bull[1] before breakfast every morning, I said, "We should do *Breakfast with the Pope*." The team thought I was joking and pooh-poohed the idea.

I let it go. But over the next month I became convinced that the idea was sound. At the February meeting I told the team I wanted us to publish the book. I wanted it available for sale in September 1995 because John Paul was coming to the United States in October. That promised good sales.

The team was stupefied. "We could never meet that deadline," said one editor. "It would take a proofreader a week just to check it." "I'll proofread it myself in two hours," I said. "I just saved a week. Let's figure out how we can make it happen."

I asked eight freelance editors to provide me with twenty diverse and readable short excerpts from John Paul II's writings. By the first week of March I had received one hundred twenty usable selections. I arranged them in random order, and *Breakfast with the Pope* was conceived.

In the 1990s the media generally accepted that papal documents were in the public domain. That meant publishers could quote them in print without permission of the Vatican. But for this important book Servant Publications needed to be sure that this was the case. We checked with other Catholic publishers that assured us that we did not need approvals. To be certain we consulted Archbishop John Foley at the Vatican communications office and asked him if we were clear to publish the book.

Weeks rolled by with no response from the archbishop. "All of Rome must be on summer holiday," I thought. Anxiety took hold as we realized that the book must get to the printer before August or we would not have books for the papal visit. All our extra effort would have been wasted.

At 6 a.m. one morning in July, feeling something like exasperation and pressure, I prayed: "Lord, I need Archbishop Foley's letter today. Let it be coming off my fax machine when I am done praying."

As I walked across the family room to my office, the fax began to buzz. It was the letter! The archbishop said we needed no permission to publish *Breakfast with the Pope*. The Lord had made me wait for his response, but he came through. He was training me in both patience and expectant faith for my needs.

I would mislead you if I did not admit that more than half the time my prayers for such things go unanswered. But that does not stop my telling God what I think I need. I know that his love for me is all-inclusive. He cares for everything about me and knows how to give me what I really need. When answers don't come I remind myself of something that C. S. Lewis once said: we will spend a lot of time in eternity thanking God for those prayers of ours he did not answer.

But answers to prayers for lesser needs expand our confidence to pray for greater concerns. We want a son freed of an addiction, a relative's broken marriage restored, or a financially ruined friend back on track. We must not let fear or false humility prevent us from presenting such needs to the Lord. Perhaps the hardest matter for us to pray for is physical healing. Let's take reflection on prayer for healing as a model for praying for any serious concern.

## Praying for Healing

Scripture and the church teach us that God cares for our health and provides for our healing. Just scan the Gospel of Matthew and track the innumerable healings Jesus performed as signs of the arrival of the kingdom. "Jesus went about all the cities and villages," says Matthew, "teaching in their synagogues, and proclaiming the good news of the kingdom, and curing every disease and every sickness" (Matt. 9:35). Jesus handed on the authority and power for healing to his apostles (see Matt. 10:1).And they empowered their successors under the guidance of the Holy Spirit.

Over the centuries the church continued to minister healing through the saints and sacraments. The prayers of saints and holy men such as Vincent Ferrer (ca. 1350–1416) and Solanus Casey (1870–1957) brought healing to hundreds of sick people. For centuries the church practiced the sacrament of extreme unction, which was specially used to prepare people for death. With the liturgical renewal after the Second Vatican Council, the church reformed the rite of the sacrament and renamed it anointing of the sick. Now it is clear that the sacrament offers spiritual and physical healing for the very ill, the aged, and those near death.

Abuses in the public healing ministry have persuaded authors like Philip Yancey to discourage people from praying for

94

### A Healing Proclaimed

Several times a year in our parish we have anointing of the sick in a communal setting . . . One of the most powerful of these celebrations occurred because of the witness of a young man who had experienced what can only be described as a miraculous recovery through the anointing of the sick and the prayers and fasting of the people of the parish as he hovered near death over a period of months. Even if he survived he was never to have walked again. A year later, during a parish celebration of anointing of the sick, he crossed the sanctuary of the church, walking with crutches, and proclaimed the first reading of the service, which was from the prophet Isaiah:

> Strengthen the weak hands,
>> and make firm the feeble knees.
> Say to those who are of a fearful heart,
>> "Be strong, do not fear!
> Here is your God.
>> He will come with vengeance,
> with terrible recompense.
>> He will come and save you."
> Then the eyes of the blind shall be opened,
>> and the ears of the deaf unstopped;
> then the lame shall leap like a deer,
>> and the tongue of the speechless sing for joy (Isa. 35:3–6).

—Rev. Robert D. Lunsford, "Through This Holy Anointing—
Then and Now," *God's Word Today*[2]

miraculous healings.[3] That's understandable, because some irresponsible televangelists, traveling ministers, and misguided Christians glibly promise healings if people will demonstrate their faith with some action. I have attended healing meetings where hundreds of parents under such pressure stripped braces and removed crutches from their children and urged them to walk, with no success. At one of these gatherings someone testified to a healing of colorblindness, but no one was healed of paralysis or other serious illness. People leave such services disappointed, angry, and embittered with God.

I appreciate the profound compassion that led Philip Yancey to caution against praying for the healing of incurable diseases. I agree with his advice on healing prayer, which is wise and practical: do not expect a miracle as an entitlement; use the healing built into our bodies and advances in medicine; don't blame God for causing suffering; and be prepared that physical healing may not take place.[4] But rather than cautioning people not to pray for miracles of healing, I think we should encourage people to pray for healing with trust and expectation.

### Trust

God enfolds us in his love. He knows everything about us— every thought before we think, every word before we speak, every deed before we act, and every need before we are aware of it (see Psalm 139). The God who watches over us, who sees us when we sit, stand, walk, or lie down, is aware of even the smallest things we need or want. We can count on him to care for us. With verses from the psalms, I remind myself daily that I am in God's hands. A line from Psalm 143 has become a theme for me: "Let dawn bring news of your faithful love, for I place my trust in you; show me the road I must travel for you to relieve my heart" (Ps. 143:8 NJB).

### Expectation

We should ask the Lord for healing of our illnesses and expect him to favor our request. The New Testament message assures us that the good things the Father will give us when we ask include healing. At the same time we must rely on God to respond to our prayer on his terms. His answer may be better or different than what we wanted. Or he may remain silent and count on us to trust him.

## God-Enhanced Natural Healing

By some grace early in our marriage, Mary Lou and I adopted the trust-and-expect approach to healing prayer. Our seven children suffered the normal share of youthful illnesses and accidents. If we missed a month at the emergency room, on our next visit the nurses would ask where we had been. When a child became sick or was injured, we would immediately pray with laying on of hands. Then we would get the appropriate help of a doctor or dispense the appropriate medicine. Although we have only anecdotal evidence, we recall that our family members often healed faster than we anticipated. I think that the Holy Spirit responded to our prayer by accelerating the healing processes of our bodies and by enhancing the doctors' techniques.

We remember one healing that resembles a miracle. One afternoon our six-year-old daughter screamed as she fell from a swing. We ran from the house to aid her, but with fright saw that our two-year-old son was drinking from a can of charcoal lighter fluid. You can imagine our fear for our son's life! We prayed over the child while we rushed him to the emergency room. The medical staff affirmed that he had drunk some of the fluid, but determined that somehow he had been spared its usual poisonous effects. And a spray of Bactine and a Band-Aid had taken care of our daughter's scraped knee. God seemed to have had the whole event in his care, even letting our daughter's cry signal us that our son was in danger.

I have never witnessed a miraculous healing of an incurable disease, but I have not shut the door on the possibility. I have experienced God's curing people of serious illnesses by employing both the healing agents he planted in our bodies and also the gifts of highly skilled physicians. For example, over the past ten years my friends Patricia and Richard Easton have suffered life-threatening bouts of cancer. They engaged the care of top-notch physicians who ranked among the best in their fields. They wrapped themselves in prayer. They had the sacrament of the anointing of the sick before every surgery and procedure. They asked the intercession of their good friend and miracle worker, St. Anthony of Padua. I and many others prayed for them every day for years. Once at Mass on a pilgrimage to Fatima, Richard heard in his heart an assurance that his wife would be healed. After surgeries, chemotherapy, and radiation, Patricia and Richard are both clear of the disease. So the "miracle" continues. God did not cure my friends with a miracle of healing, but he responded to our prayer by making them well through human means.

Maybe we will never see a miracle that overturns the laws of nature. But with faithful prayer we may experience God bringing healing through the body's natural processes and the hands of medical professionals.

### Interpreting God's Answers

I have prayed for the physical healing of many people who did not get well. I had expected the Lord to heal them. But when they did not recover, I had to trust that he permitted something better than what I had asked. Or he had allowed something I did not yet understand and would have to endure.

In 1973 my mother was afflicted with breast cancer. My two sisters and I entrusted her to the Lord, expecting him to heal her. But she died two years later. As I reflected on this experience, I realized that God had given my mother a spiritual healing, by releasing her from the problem of anger. I wrote about it in an earlier book:

> Mother had a great, simple faith, and she did many things well. But handling her anger was one thing she did badly. Lifelong she grappled with suppressed anger, irritability, occasional outbursts, and above all, resentments.
>
> Mother was one of the younger daughters of a second generation Italian family, a factor that occasioned much of the anger that plagued her last years. For instance, daughters in families like hers customarily never left home until they married. But when both of my sisters turned twenty, they moved out on their own to pursue careers, and Mother resented it profoundly.
>
> For a year before Mother died cancer eroded her body. Shortly after it was diagnosed she received the sacrament of the anointing of the sick . . . We hoped that the sacrament and our prayers would heal her of the disease and spare her life.
>
> But to our disappointment, Mother did not receive a physical healing . . . However, the Lord healed her soul: he cured completely the anger that had gnawed at her and poisoned her relationships with my sisters. She who for years had roiled with anger and resentment became fundamentally peaceful. No one had to persuade her or counsel her . . . Before Mother died she reconciled with her daughters and spent several happy months with them at her side.[5]

I believe that God's curing my mother's anger prepared her for her eternal life with him. I have accepted that as his answer to my prayer for her healing. This experience has become a lens that clarifies my scrutiny of answered prayer. It helps me see more clearly how God has chosen to respond to my request and to accept his answer as grace.

But what am I to make of a case when I have prayed for a healing and not only does God fail to provide something better, but also he seems not to answer at all? For example, I have prayed faithfully for friends with Alzheimer's disease and lung cancer, and those illnesses worsened until my friends died. Unanswered prayers like these tested my dependence on the Lord, but they did not fracture it. They led me to look for truths that would strengthen my resolve to rely on God.

### Facing Unanswered Prayer

How long, Yahweh, will you forget me? For ever?
How long will you turn away your face from me?
How long must I nurse rebellion in my soul,
sorrow in my heart day and night?
How long is the enemy to domineer over me?

Look down, answer me, Yahweh my God!
Give light to my eyes or I shall fall into the sleep of death.
Or my foe will boast, 'I have overpowered him,'
and my enemy have the joy of seeing me stumble.

As for me, I trust in your faithful love, Yahweh.
Let my heart delight in your saving help,
let me sing to Yahweh for his generosity to me,
let me sing to the name of Yahweh the Most High!

—Psalm 13 NJB

I have found some comforting perspectives in the letters of St. Paul. He believed in physical healing and miracles and even raised a young man from the dead (see 1 Cor. 12: 9–10 and Acts 20:9–11). But although he presumably prayed for them, Paul's friends who were sick were not always healed. For instance, he directed Timothy, his coworker, to drink a little wine for the sake of his problems with digestion and frequent ailments (see 1 Tim. 5:23). On one of his missionary journeys he had to leave behind Trophimus, another colleague, because of sickness (see 2 Tim. 4:20). A serious illness compelled Paul himself to stay at Galatia for an extended time (see Gal. 4:10–12). These situations did not frustrate Paul. His example of moving ahead with consistent faith encourages me to do the same when I face unanswered prayers.

Saint Paul also explains why some prayers for physical healing do not receive the desired answer. When Jesus came to redeem us he demonstrated God's saving grace with healings and raising people from the dead. But St. Paul says that we still suffer sickness and death because we have yet to receive the fullness of our salvation. "We ourselves, who have the first fruits of the Spirit, groan inwardly while we wait for adoption, the redemption of our bodies. For in hope we were saved. Now hope that is seen is not hope. For who hopes for what is seen? But if we hope for what we do not see, we wait for it with patience" (Rom. 8:23–24). This Pauline perspective enables me to be thankful when a healing prayer is answered, and patient and still trustful when it is not.

Jesus himself modeled trust in the face of unanswered prayer. Distressed by fear of his coming death, he prayed, "My Father, if it is possible, let this cup pass from me" (Matt. 26:39). When God did not respond, the Lord humbly embraced his fate. From the cross he prayed Psalm 22, lamenting his Father's abandoning him. "My God, my God, why have you forsaken me? Why are you so far from helping me?" he asked (Ps. 22:1). Although the Lord prayed these words to express his painful feelings, they lead up to his declaring his unshaken confidence in God. Like many other Old Testament songs, Psalm 22 begins with cries to God who offers no help, but climaxes with praises for his ultimate deliverance. With death approaching, Jesus affirmed with the psalm his reliance on his Father: "You who fear the LORD, praise him! . . . For he did not despise or abhor the affliction of the afflicted; he did not hide his face from me, but heard when I cried to him" (Ps. 22:23, 24). When all seems lost, we can find a glimmer of hope in the Lord's example.

What's more, we can look to the cross for comfort when God remains silent to our pleas for healing. In our misery we can behold Jesus, the Son of God and the Son of Mary, hanging there in dreadful agony. If we look closely we can catch a glimpse of Christ joining us in our suffering. We see the Word made flesh taking on extreme human suffering. God who suffered as a man now suffers in us when we are ill or injured. We may have to endure the hardship of chronic or incurable physical illness in ourselves or loved ones. That is a rough road rutted with pain and grief. But with the Lord as our companion and with his support we can find strength for our difficult journey.

I have found that daily prayer strengthens my reliance on God, just as my daily two-mile walk invigorates my body. I recommend both practices. Every morning we should offer ourselves to the Lord, framing our lives with trust.

Think
- Do you believe that God loves you?
- Do you believe that he cares for you and provides for your needs and wants?
- Do you pray for needs expecting God to answer you?
- When have you experienced answered prayers?
- Has God ever given you something better than what you asked for?
- Do you pray for major things like physical healing?

Pray

Take fifteen minutes to pray and consider the following:

- How do you respond when God does not answer your prayers?
- What perspective might help you handle unanswered prayer more effectively?
- On a scale of 1 to 5, 5 being the highest, how would you rank your reliance on God?
- What one step might you take to increase your trust in God?

Act
- Select one action that occurred to you during your prayer time.
- Determine the best way to implement it in your life and practice it for a month. At the end of the month, evaluate your experience. If you found it helpful, continue it. If not, try another approach.

# 9

## Praying for Others

I typically conclude my daily morning prayer with intercessions. I take about ten minutes to pray for family, friends, the sick, people who have asked me for prayer, and people that the Holy Spirit has brought to my attention. I entrust each person to the care of the Lord, who knows better than I do what each one needs most. I regard this intercessory prayer as part of my commitment as a follower of Christ. I see it as way of drawing others close to the Lord, which is my responsibility as his disciple.

### The Prayer of Disciples

I have prayed the Our Father often since my childhood, but only lately have I realized what I was getting myself into. We call it "The Lord's Prayer." But I think we might also name it "The Disciple's Prayer," because each time we pray it we renew our commitment to follow the Lord and work with him. "Thy kingdom come," we pray, affirming our decision to collaborate with him to advance God's kingdom. "Thy will be done," we pray, avowing that we want to make his loving presence recognized everywhere. Thus, by praying the Our Father we obligate ourselves anew to help him rescue our fellows from the dark regions of sin, sickness, and death. We resolve to fulfill the terms of our discipleship—to proclaim the good news, to teach by word and example Christ's new way of living, and to bring healing, both physical and spiritual, to others.

Jesus implemented his threefold strategy of preaching, teaching, and healing by prayer and action. He expects his disciples to imitate his approach. We can observe the Lord's methods in St. Paul, one of his premier disciples. Paul worked ceaselessly to bring people into the kingdom. But he undergirded his relentless activity with equally relentless intercession, both for conversion of nonbelievers and also for the perseverance of new Christians. For twenty-first century disciples, prayer and action are still our tools for doing Christ's work of evangelization.

I believe that the Lord wants us to take a concern for people close to us, to pray for them, and to do all that we can to draw them closer to him. In my daily prayer I try to follow the example of Paul, who always remembered to pray for those given to his care. For instance, I imitate his prayers for the Ephesians and the Colossians. I pray for family, relatives, friends, and acquaintances that they may know the will of God and come to live lives pleasing to him, bearing good fruit in good works, growing in knowledge of God, and receiving the grace to persevere (see Col. 1:9–12).

**Paul's Prayers**

I do not cease to give thanks for you as I remember you in my prayers. I pray that the God of our Lord Jesus Christ, the Father of glory, may give you a spirit of wisdom and revelation as you come to know him, so that, with the eyes of your heart enlightened, you may know what is the hope to which he has called you, what are the riches of his glorious inheritance among the saints, and what is the immeasurable greatness of his power for us who believe, according to the working of his great power.

—Ephesians 1:16–19

For this reason I bow my knees before the Father, from whom every family in heaven and on earth takes its name. I pray that, according to the riches of his glory, he may grant that you may be strengthened in your inner being with power through his Spirit, and that Christ may dwell in your hearts through faith, as you are being rooted and grounded in love. I pray that you may have the power to comprehend, with all the saints, what is the breadth and length and height and depth, and to know the love of Christ that surpasses knowledge, so that you may be filled with all the fullness of God.

Now to him who by the power at work within us is able to accomplish abundantly far more than all we can ask or imagine, to him be glory in the church and in Christ Jesus to all generations, forever and ever. Amen.

—Ephesians 3:14–21

## A Routine of Intercession

I made the decision to pray daily for others as a response to my experience on a Cursillo weekend. The Cursillo is a "short course" in Christian living.[1] I attended the first South Bend, Indiana, Cursillo in the winter of 1963, shortly after enrolling in graduate school at Notre Dame. The weekend had a profound effect on me. Spontaneous prayer with others, a hallmark of the Cursillo, made me more sensitive to the presence of Jesus in ordinary circumstances. I also realized the joy that could come from collaborating with others to spread the good news. The Cursillo also taught me practical lessons, especially how to intercede for others.

Legislators and government officials from the state of Michigan presented South Bend's first Cursillo. Michigan's attorney general, a gentle but strong Christian, led the group at my table. Toward the end of the weekend he gave a talk titled "Environments" that presented a strategy for praying for people in our various social groups. He explained that we all live within a series of concentric social circles, widening out from family to relatives, neighbors, friends, coworkers or fellow students, companions in our church community, clerks at stores we frequent, casual acquaintances, and so on. This was the heart of his message: we should prepare for the work of evangelization by deciding always to share our faith experience with others in our social circles when they give us an opening; we should be praying regularly for the people in all of these environments; and we should let the Holy Spirit create opportunities for us to help someone in one of these circles draw closer to Christ.

That seemed easy enough, and in my eagerness I said I'd do it. So I identified the people in my environments. I began praying daily, circle by social circle. I started a routine of intercession then that I still follow today.

## Early Successes

I have enjoyed noteworthy answers to these intercessory prayers. Some of the more dramatic experiences occurred from 1967 to 1974 during my tenure as a history professor at Grand Valley State College, near Grand Rapids, Michigan. At that time I was also leading a city-wide charismatic prayer meeting in Grand Rapids.

As a state-supported liberal arts college, Grand Valley maintained concern about separation of church and state. I knew that I had to take great care about when and how I might speak to a student about Christ and the church. I qualified my decisions about evangelization: I would pray for my students. I would not initiate faith conversations, but when a student gave me an opening, I would respond with testimony or teaching.

I did do a few things that facilitated student-initiated discussions of faith matters. For example, I wove Catholic perspectives into my freshman Western civilization course. I also became faculty adviser simultaneously to the Catholic student parish and the Intervarsity Christian Fellowship, an evangelical outreach. This made students wonder how I could relate to groups that stood at opposite ends of the Christian spectrum. When asked I would explain: "I'm comfortable with both Catholics and evangelicals. I'm an evangelical Catholic or a Catholic evangelical, however you want to put it, because I believe in the Jesus of the Gospels." My ploy opened some good evangelistic conversations.

I have some evidence that my tactics worked. For example, years later at a conference a young priest tapped me on the shoulder and greeted me. "Professor Ghezzi," he said, addressing me with a title I had shed long before. "You may not remember me, but I was an atheist in your Western Civ. class that we all called 'Catholicism 101.' You took me to a charismatic prayer meeting, and I secretly thought you were nuts." He told me that my teaching and interest in him had ultimately played a part in his spiritual journey.

My first noteworthy success occurred early in my career at Grand Valley. One day in 1968, Ray, a very enthusiastic stu-

## Witness and Words

Above all the Gospel must be proclaimed by witness. Take a Christian or a handful of Christians who, in the midst of their own community, show their capacity for understanding and acceptance, their sharing of life and destiny with other people, . . . Let us suppose that . . . they radiate in an altogether simple and unaffected way their faith in values that go beyond current values, and their hope in something that is not seen . . .

Through this wordless witness these Christians stir up irresistible questions in the hearts of those who see how they live: Why are they like this? . . .What or who is it that inspires them? Why are they in our midst? Such a witness is already a silent proclamation of the Good News and a very powerful and effective one. Here we have an initial act of evangelization . . .

Nevertheless this always remains insufficient, because even the finest witness will prove ineffective in the long run if it is not explained, justified—what Peter called always having "your answer ready for people who ask you the reason for the hope that you all have" (see 1 Pet 3:15)—and made explicit by a clear and unequivocal proclamation of the Lord Jesus. The Good News proclaimed by the witness of life sooner or later has to be proclaimed by the word of life. There is no true evangelization if the name, the teaching, the life, the promises, the kingdom and the mystery of Jesus of Nazareth, the Son of God are not proclaimed.

—Pope Paul VI (1897–1978), *Evangelization in the Modern World*[2]

dent, burst into my office. "Professor Ghezzi," he said, "my high school teachers told me that unless I meet my professors I will get lost in the crowd and my college education will not be as good as it could have been. I'm in your Western Civ. class. So I'm here to get to know you." Was that an opening, or what? I said under my breath, "Ray, you asked for it." Then I proceeded to give him my testimony about how I came to commit my life to Christ and experience a release of the Holy Spirit. Ray took it all in, laughing uneasily a few times. He may have been a little stunned by my openness, but he just asked a few questions and left.

The following Monday morning Ray came back, more excited than the first time. "You won't believe what happened! Well, maybe you will! On Friday night I stayed in my room and really prayed to know God, and I experienced God's love for me more than I ever have—I got baptized in the Spirit." Thus began my long friendship with Ray. He accompanied me to prayer meetings and later received the gift of tongues. He returned to the Catholic Church. He became a leader in the Catholic student parish. He lived with my family a short time before he ventured off to do lay missionary work on a reservation in South Dakota. Ray's story counts as answered prayer, don't you think??

Encouraged by that success, I continued to pray for my students with even greater confidence. About a year later, on the first day of class, I noticed Tom seated in the front row. To my alarm I immediately sensed the Holy Spirit say, "I want you to tell that young man that I love him and want him to come to know me." *Yeah, sure!* I thought. *A teacher in a state college is going to behave unprofessionally and accost a student with that message!* So I prayed, "Lord, if this is you leading me, you are going to have to bring that student into my life." With that I thought I was pretty safe.

But that very afternoon Tom came to my office, handed me a pink card, and said, "Professor Ghezzi, the dean has appointed you as my faculty adviser. And I need some advice." You might think that I would have got the message and told Tom what the Holy Spirit had said. But no, my timidity froze my tongue on this first encounter, and on the second as well. The third time Tom dropped by my office, I took a deep breath, got up from my desk, closed the door, and said, "Tom, I don't know how you are going to take this. The first time I saw you in class I sensed God saying that I should tell you that he loves you and wants you to come to know him."

I thought Tom might look at me as though I were crazy, turn, and leave. But his unexpected response was, "Why didn't you tell me sooner. I needed to hear that." I could tell that he was not criticizing me for my delay, but was simply stating a fact. In the next few weeks we had some long conversations about the Lord and the Christian life. Tom's evening schedule prevented him from attending prayer meetings. So Ray, several other students, and I arranged a Tuesday afternoon faith sharing group just for him. We met every week for a year and watched Tom respond to the Holy Spirit's invitation to come to know God. About three months along he came to me and said, "I shouldn't be living with my girlfriend, should I?" "Probably not," I said. So he ended the relationship. Later, he married Ann, who shared his Christian commitment. They have served as leaders in their Pentecostal church for more than thirty years.

These early successes confirmed my decision to pray faithfully for others, and I have made it a daily habit.

## The List

In order to reinforce my sieve-like memory, for many years I have kept a list of people tucked into my Bible. On it I have arranged names and intentions that I want to bring to the Lord's attention. The list contains the names of my family members, relatives, friends, the sick, coworkers, prisoners, priests, ministries, and people in a few other categories. Ray, Tom, and their families still appear there. Every morning at the close of my prayer time I pray through the list, mentioning specific needs as they come to mind. "Let the Holy Spirit encourage Tyler and Mark," I might pray. "Have mercy, Lord, on all those imprisoned at Lake Correctional Institute, and heal Patty of the cancer that has invaded her body."

I have also placed a number of people I don't know well on my list. For example, I believe the Holy Spirit led me to add a poet from Great Britain that I met on an airplane, a grocery store cashier that lost her job and moved away, and a student that helped me at a conference.

I also pray for people who have hurt me in some way. Daily I ask the Lord to give them every blessing. Praying represents my forgiving of them and keeps my heart clear of ill feelings toward them.

I expect that the Lord hears and answers my prayers for all the people on my list. In most cases, I have no way of learning what he has done. But occasionally I discover answered prayers. Let me tell you about a few of them.

I met Daiva nearly twenty years ago. She came to Ann Arbor from Lithuania for major surgery on her legs that would enable her to walk and live a normal life. My friend Rosaleen cared for Daiva in her home and asked me to pray, which I have done daily. Today she has an advanced degree, a good job, and a lovely adopted daughter.

Mike came into my life four decades ago when he was a student at Grand Valley State College. He has held a spot on the list all these years. Mike lived with my family for seven years, became a Catholic, married a lovely woman, endured the tragic death of a daughter, and has become a deacon in his parish.

I prayed for my friends Dick and Patty Easton through serious bouts with cancer (See page 98). They are now cancer free. Also in remission from cancer are my friend Myra and a friend who is a priest.

My cousin Pam appears on the list. I prayed for her through a difficult divorce and through a job change, which has lifted her spirits. Recently, she told me that she is full of joy. Others on the list have found jobs, but I am still praying for many out-of-work friends.

Some inactive Catholics that I prayed for have returned to the church, including a celebrity movie star, who now prays and goes to Mass every day. These Catholic "reverts" increase my faith for the many that I hope to evangelize.

Now, did my prayers cause God to intervene in these lives? No way. The Holy Spirit gets full credit for the changes, healings, and improvements. Did my prayers make any contribution to these lives that God has blessed? I like to think so, but I have no proof. However, I continue to pray every day for every person on my list because I am confident that God hears and responds with grace.

## Praying for Family

Mary Lou and I have seven adult children, six of whom are married, and fifteen grandchildren. Along with Mary Lou, our family occupies the top spot on my list. Every day I pray confidently that each will come to know, love, and serve the Lord and be with him forever. In the 1980s and 1990s I wrote and spoke extensively about keeping kids Catholic. As some of my own children drifted away from the church, I focused my prayer squarely on their salvation in Christ.

I pray for my family with complete confidence. I am convinced that God always says yes to parents' prayers for the salvation of their children. I believe that he cannot say no to such prayers because to do so would contradict his divine will.

Scripture and the church explain that God created human beings because he wanted them in his own family. The Lord's desire to have us with him as his children runs as a theme through the New Testament. For example, St. John says that to all who receive Jesus and believe in his name, he gives power to become children of God (see John 1:12). Paul also makes it clear that God's plan is inclusive: "I urge that supplications, prayers, intercessions, and thanksgivings be made for everyone . . . This is right and is acceptable in the sight of God our Savior, who desires everyone to be saved and to come to the knowledge of the truth" (1 Tim. 2:1, 3–4). My reflection on such passages has persuaded me that the Lord wants my kids in his family even more than I do.

Jesus's repeated promise to do whatever we ask in his name has galvanized my conviction (see sidebar). When we pray in Jesus's name we are not repeating a formula

## Jesus's Promises

I will do whatever you ask in my name, so that the Father may be glorified in the Son. If in my name you ask me for anything, I will do it.

—John 14:13–14

If you abide in me, and my words abide in you, ask for whatever you wish, and it will be done for you.

—John 15:7

And I appointed you to go and bear fruit, fruit that will last, so that the Father will give you whatever you ask him in my name.

—John 15:16

Very truly, I tell you, if you ask anything of the Father in my name, he will give it to you.

—John 16:23

Ask, and it will be given you; search, and you will find; knock, and the door will be opened for you. For everyone who asks receives, and everyone who searches finds, and for everyone who knocks, the door will be opened.

—Matthew 7:7–8

required for answered prayer. Tacking "in Jesus's name" onto a request does not guarantee that God will say yes. Rather we are invoking the very presence of God and praying in accord with his will. Because he determined to adopt us as children even before time began (see Eph. 1:1–5), his desire to have a family corresponds to the heart of his nature—his unchangeable will for human beings. Thus I believe that when I ask him in Jesus's name to welcome my children, their spouses, and my grandchildren into his family, he says, "Yes, of course, that's just what I want."

I know that God will give my children and their families every opportunity and grace to turn their lives over to him. But he will not override their freedom. They must decide to accept his invitations themselves. And I must use my witness and words to persuade them to act.

If you could look over my shoulder and scan my intercessory list, you might be surprised to find yourself there. Every day I ask the Holy Spirit to strengthen my readers, bringing them whatever graces they may need for the day and for their lives.

Think

- How often do you pray for others?
- Do you pray for family, relatives, and friends?
- When you pray for others, what do you ask the Lord to do for them?
- Do you pray for the salvation and conversion of people in your social environments?
- Do you pray for opportunities to share your faith with others?

Pray

Take fifteen minutes to pray and consider the following:

- If you are not interceding daily for others, consider identifying the people you should be praying for.
- If you are already praying for others, consider what you might do to pray more effectively. Are there some additional people you should be praying for?

Act

- If you have not been praying for others regularly, make a mental or hard-copy list of people in your social circles that you want to pray for. Build five minutes for intercessory prayer into your daily routine.
- If you have been praying for others, implement actions that occurred to you when you prayed about their needs.
- If you pray for evangelistic opportunities, be ready to speak to others about how you came to know the Lord and to make a commitment to him.
- Keep your eyes and ears open for answered prayers.

# 10

## Praying with Others

I have already told how praying with others prepared me for personal daily prayer. Joining friends for morning prayer at Duquesne University not only taught me to pray but also introduced me to the realities of the body of Christ and the communion of saints. Now, five decades later, although I am physically alone at prayer, I know I am praying in community with the Trinity, with the saints and angels, and with friends that I have agreed to join daily. This is the mature fruit of seeds that were planted in me as a child.

I attended daily Mass as a boy, but not because of some precocious devotion typical of a child saint like Dominic Savio (1842–57). The eight o'clock Mass at our local parish served as childcare for me and my friends before school started at nine. I don't count it as my first experience of praying with others, since I did not realize what was going on. I'm sure that I didn't pray. I don't remember much about these times except that our pastor could breeze through the Latin prayers in eighteen minutes flat. I recall most clearly the day that Sister Wallburga corrected me with a rap of her ruler for kneeling with my backside slouched against the pew. I have knelt up straight ever since, and have to resist rapping slouchers on the shoulder and telling them to do the same.

Although I was unaware of it, something very significant was going on at Mass. Represented by the priest, Christ was offering himself to the Father. Little did I realize that as a member of Christ's body, the Lord included me in his life-giving prayer.

### Praying with Christ

Not until I awakened to all things Christian in my late teens did I grasp the reality of the body of Christ. I don't remember my first exposure to the ancient doctrine. But early in my college career I read the encyclical letter of Pope Pius XII (1878–1958), entitled *Mystici Corporis Christi* ("On the Mystical Body of Christ"). Although the pope had written the document in dense "papalese," I read it like headline news—I got the message. Jesus had fulfilled his promise that he would be *in* me and I would be *in* him, just as he was *in* his Father (see John 14:20).

St. Paul explained how the Lord made this happen. He arranged to continue his presence among us as a corporate body—the church—a living organism of which he would be the head and we the members (see 1 Cor. 12:27; Eph. 4:4–16). Jesus used the image of a vine and branches to describe how it was to work. His divine life would animate each of his members just as plant life animated each branch, stem, leaf, and berry of a vine (see John 15:4–6). "Christ our Lord," said Pope Pius XII, "wills the Church to live his own supernatural life,

### Living in Christ

I will not leave you orphaned; I am coming to you. In a little while the world will no longer see me, but you will see me; because I live, you also will live. On that day you will know that I am in my Father, and you in me, and I in you.

—John 14:18–20

How can one being live in another? . . .

Our Lord speaks constantly of our living in him. There is then a twofold *in*. He must live in us. We must live in him . . .

Somehow . . . we must be in Christ as the cells are in our own body: then Christ will live in us as we live in our bodily cells . . . Christ, living on this earth, had a human body in which he worked among men . . . He has left the earth; he is eternally in heaven at the right hand of the Father; but he still works among men in his body, no longer his *natural body*, the body that was brought into being in the womb of Mary by the power of the Holy Spirit, but in his *Mystical Body*, the Church, the body that was brought into being in the Upper Room after his Ascension by the power of the Holy Spirit.

The Church, then, is his Body, linked to him really, organically, inseparably, as a body to its head: his life flows through the Church as my life flows through my body . . . And as I live in the individual cells of my body, so he lives in the individual cells of his Body.

—Frank J. Sheed (1897–1981), *A Map of Life*[1]

and by his divine power permeates his whole body and nourishes and sustains each of the members . . . in the same way as the vine nourishes and makes fruitful the branches which are joined to it."[2]

The doctrine of the body of Christ came to life for me among my friends at Duquesne. I saw how faculty and students generously gave their time, energy, and money to extend the Lord's earthly ministry. For example, some worked to bring relief to the poor and others to advance the causes of racial justice and Christian unity.

Most of all I experienced my participation in Christ's body when I gathered with others for prayer. I realized at morning prayer with Chi Rho and at noon Mass with the university community that something extraordinary happened for me—something supernatural. From his place in heaven Jesus was praying, and as the head he was praying in and through all of us, the members of his body. By a special working that we call the liturgy, the Lord had arranged for me to join his never-ending prayer that echoes through the universe. Morning prayer took on a deeper meaning for me, the psalms were more beautiful, the Scripture more pertinent. I delighted in uniting my prayer with his and that of millions of saints in heaven and millions on earth.

I also celebrated the great privilege he granted me at Mass. Christ himself through the priest was representing his once-for-all sacrificial death that wiped away our sins and repaired our relationship with God. And he allowed me to offer myself as part of his sacrifice.

Joining the prayer of Christ and his body in the liturgy has benefited me now for decades. The power of praying in Christ has spilled over into my relationships and daily prayer.

## Praying with Others

My first experience of praying spontaneously with others occurred in 1962. Professor Storey took me and several other students to Philadelphia to attend a conference on liturgical renewal. I had looked forward to the conference because I wanted to learn more about worship. I also wanted to hear about reforms of the liturgy that the bishops might consider at the Second Vatican Council, which had just opened. Although I don't remember any of the conference sessions, I recall praying late one night in our hotel room with Dr. Storey, my friend Jack, and two other students. Each of us prayed aloud, addressing the Lord in our own words. We praised him, thanked him for his grace and gifts, and asked him to care for our needs. Jesus must have been standing by just waiting for us to open our mouths, because as soon as we began to pray he flooded the room with his presence. I sensed that he moved among us as we prayed and deepened our friendship with him and with each other.

Back at Duquesne we introduced the practice of informal prayer to Chi Rho. It soon became a regular feature of our meetings and social gatherings. For example, at our New Year's

### Prayer and Friendship

It is no small consolation in this life to have someone who can unite with you in an intimate affection and the embrace of a holy love. Someone in whom your spirit can rest, to whom you can pour out your soul, to whose pleasant exchanges, as to soothing songs, you can fly in sorrow. To the dear breast of whose friendship, amidst the many troubles of the world, you can safely retire. A person who can shed tears with you in your worries, be happy with you when things go well, search out with you the answers to your problems, whom with the ties of charity you can lead into the depths of your heart. A person who, though absent in body, is yet present in spirit, where heart to heart you can talk to him, where the sweetness of the Spirit flows between you, where you so join yourself and cleave to him that soul mingles with soul and two become one.

And so praying to Christ for your friend, and longing to be heard by Christ for your friend's sake, you reach out with devotion and desire to Christ himself. And suddenly and insensibly, as though touched by the gentleness of Christ close at hand, you begin to taste how sweet he is and to feel how lovely he is. Thus from that holy love with which you embrace your friend, you rise to that love by which you embrace Christ.

—Aelred of Rievaulx (1110–67), *Spiritual Friendship*[3]

Eve parties first we prayed, then we popped the champagne and exchanged hugs all around.

As I reflected on the impact that spontaneous prayer had on us, I observed that it created openness in people both to the Lord and to Christian relationships. Praying aloud with others made people aware of Jesus as a person who loved them. The experience moved them along the way to giving their lives to him. And it bonded them with brothers and sisters in his body.

Later the spiritual effectiveness of the Cursillo's group dynamics confirmed my observation.[4] For example, during a men's Cursillo weekend the participants, many of whom have only a casual relationship with the Lord, are given the opportunity to pray spontaneously with others. This is a novel, even revolutionary, experience for many attendees, who are more accustomed to praying even formal prayers privately. A leader tells them that he is going to pass a crucifix around and invites them to pray aloud at their turn. He assures the men that they don't have to pray if they choose not to. Then he prays, setting an example, and hands the crucifix to the man next to him. Most men pray aloud, and I suspect that they feel the Lord drawing them. This prayer time is a turning point for most participants, preparing them to commit themselves to Christ. After the weekend, the men meet weekly in groups where after study and sharing they may pray informally.

Informal prayer with others has become a mainstay for me, enriching my relationship with the Lord and with my friends. Recently, for example, I visited with Brandon, an enthusiastic and gifted young Catholic. We talked about family, the imminent birth of his first son, books, the art of writing, and his blog piece about racial justice.[5] At the end of our conversation we prayed. Once again, just as he had done so many times for me since that night in Philadelphia, the Lord made his presence felt between us. He was creating another bond of friendship.

## Praying Together

Mary Lou and I have benefited from our involvement in many groups that pray together. All were schools of prayer for us, each teaching or training us in some way to give ourselves more fully to God.

In the early years of our marriage, we participated in meetings of the Christian Family Movement, where we learned the value of married couples supporting each other with advice and prayer. In those groups we built lasting friendships with George and Mary Martin, Bud and Mary Lothschutz, and other couples that we are still linked with in prayer, although we now live miles apart.

We have also prayed with hundreds and sometimes thousands in charismatic renewal prayer meetings. These gatherings generate a near-tangible unity among participants who share vocal prayer, song, Scripture, spiritual gifts, and testimony. I especially enjoy the experience of worship at these meetings. I sense the Lord's presence flowing amid the chorus of voices praising him. I feel him drawing me to himself and enfolding me in his love. Praying together with others offers no better reward.

Praying as a family has been by far the most important group prayer for Mary Lou and me. We prayed simply with young children at bedtime and blessed them. As they got older we prayed with them after supper. We used songs, short scriptures, and prayer books to trigger interest and inspiration. Praying together became more challenging when our kids turned into teenagers. But we worked hard at it because we were convinced that family prayer time gave us opportunities to share our commitment to Christ with our children.

Now that our children are grown up and gone, Mary Lou and I pray evening prayer after supper. I also attend daily Mass. I worship with a faithful assembly of women and men at the 7 a.m. liturgy. Reminiscent of my boyhood experience, Fr. Tom, a retired priest who serves in our parish, can zip through the liturgy, homily and all, in eighteen minutes flat. Most of my companions are on the far side of sixty, but no one slouches against the pew. All of these early-bird worshipers seem to be engaged in Christian service. Jack and Jean lead an outreach to the families of prisoners; Chuck and Arlene teach in the adult religious education program; Larry and Rose visit the sick in hospitals, and so on. We all look out for Mel, an eighty-six-year-old retired businessman and amateur poet afflicted with Parkinson's disease who drives his motorized wheelchair to church. Praying together with these folks energizes me. I see the Lord working through them and I sense him praying through them, giving me my daily firsthand experience of the body of Christ.

Think

- What is your experience of the body of Christ?
- In what ways have you sensed Christ living in you? Do you experience him in your Christian service? In your worship and prayer?
- Do you pray together with others? In what situations?

- When have you prayed spontaneously with others? How does informal prayer affect you?
- Do you pray with your family? If so, how do you facilitate it?

Pray

Take fifteen minutes to pray and consider the following:

- If you are not praying with others, what one step might you take to build group prayer into your life?
- If you are praying with others, consider what you might do to enhance your experience.
- What opportunities do you have to pray spontaneously with others? At parish meetings? In a sharing group? With family? With a sick friend?

Act

- In the next month, select at least three opportunities to initiate or take part in informal prayer with others.
- If you have not been praying with family, begin to pray together for five minutes after supper or at bedtime. Have each person thank God for something and ask God for something. Close with the Our Father, Hail Mary, and Glory Be.
- If you have a family prayer time, decide to do one thing to renew or strengthen it.

# 11

## Faithfulness to Prayer

I describe my daily prayer as an adventure. I could also call it a habit because I have woven it into the fabric of my life. I gave up "trying" to pray daily many years ago. I discovered that if I did not build praying into my routine I routinely replaced it with lesser priorities. And as I said in a previous chapter, a whopping speeding ticket persuaded me not to schedule my prayer time while driving. I learned my lesson: give the Lord the undivided attention he deserves. I made it a rule of thumb that I can pray while driving, but I cannot drive while I am praying.

Willpower does not account for my faithfulness to daily prayer. My will is not strong enough to get me to resist a slice of carrot cake, let alone to get me on my knees every morning. Only by grace have I been able to persevere. I am convinced that the Lord is so determined to communicate with us that he lovingly woos us till we give in and start praying daily.

**Neither Rain, nor Sleet, nor Gloom of Night . . .**

After I came to Ireland—every day I had to tend sheep, and many times a day I prayed—the love of God and His fear came to me more and more, and my faith was strengthened. And my spirit was moved so that in a single day I would say as many as a hundred prayers, and almost as many in the night, and this even when I was staying in the woods and on the mountain, and I used to get up for prayer before daylight, through snow, through frost, through rain, and I felt no harm, and there was no sloth in me—as I now see, because the spirit within me was then fervent.

*—The Confession of St. Patrick* (389–461)[1]

God instills faithfulness in us by touching our hearts. The thought that the Lord of all loves me and delights in spending time with me makes me want to pray. Saint Patrick, for example, says that as a youth the love of God moved him to pray throughout the day. Like him we get the strength to persevere at daily prayer by collaborating with the Holy Spirit. Scripture teaches that faithfulness grows in us as a fruit of the Spirit (see Gal. 5:22–23). The Spirit plants the seed of fidelity in us. He motivates us to express our love for God and relate to him loyally—for example, by praying every day. If we are to bear fruit, we must act—for example, by doing our part to carry on a conversation with the Lord. Although faithfulness to daily prayer comes as a grace of the Spirit, it also requires some effort on our part. We need to open ourselves to God and wait for him to act.

It would be nice if our prayer always flowed freely. That doesn't always happen because obstacles cross our paths. Among these are distractions, dryness, and doubts. I believe God allows these hindrances to give us opportunities to grow in faithfulness. With his grace, dealing with obstacles will mature us as pray-ers and strengthen us as followers of Christ.

## Distractions

As a beginner at prayer I acquired the bad habit of evaluating my prayer times. "Well, that was a lousy experience," I would say to myself. "I bet even God was bored." Then one day it occurred to me that the Lord welcomed my prayer, no matter how poorly I expressed it, and I stopped my negative reviews. I thought that he might be pleased that at least I was showing up and making an effort to open to him.

Distractions used to frustrate me. My mind tends to stray like an undisciplined puppy, poking into all sorts of things. My attention may drift from prayer to an overdue bill, an unresolved disagreement with my wife, the plot of a novel, a broken faucet, a friend undergoing heart surgery, or a deadline looming at work. With grace and effort I have learned how to set some distractions aside and to use others to enhance my prayer.

When an idle thought pops up, something like the clever resolution of a mystery I just read, I immediately turn from it and back to the Lord. Sometimes by the turning I go a little deeper in prayer. If a family or business matter demands attention, I make a note, either mental or written, and set it aside. Sometimes I believe a thought that distracts me comes from the Holy Spirit. In such cases I take time to pray about the concern. "Lord," I might say, "help me to see Mary Lou's side of the disagreement we are having and give us the wisdom to resolve it peacefully." Or I might take a few minutes to pray for Tuggy and Raymond Dunton, who serve marginalized Native Americans throughout the United States. I accept such interruptions as little gifts of the Spirit that allow me to pray in accord with God's heart. In these ways I turn distractions into prayer enhancers.

## Dryness

On rare occasions I enjoy a sense of God's presence that takes my breath away. At other times my prayer goes dry, and I feel disconnected from him. I don't pay much attention to either extreme. I don't pursue the joyous moments, trying to make them last. I receive them as wonderful but temporary graces and move on. Nor do I worry about the dry times. I take them in stride and keep on praying. Just as I don't believe in writer's block, which I regard as an excuse for my not thinking through things, I also don't believe in pray-er's block. I cherish the faithful example of Mother Teresa (1910–97), who experienced Jesus's loving closeness when he called her to found the Mis-

---

### Praying without Feeling

Our Lord is most glad and delighted with our prayer. He looks for it, and He wills to have it, for with his gaze He makes us as like Himself in condition as we are in nature. This is His blessed will, for He says, "Pray inwardly, though you think it gives you no satisfaction. For the prayer is profitable, though you feel nothing, though you see nothing, yes, though you think you can do nothing. In dryness and in barrenness, in sickness and in feebleness—then is your prayer most pleasing to Me, though you think it gives you but little satisfaction. And so it is with all your believing prayers, in my sight."

Because of the reward and the endless thanks He will give us for it, He covets our continual prayer in His sight. God accepts the good will and the bitter labor of his servant, however we may feel. Therefore, it pleases Him that we work reasonably, with discretion, both in our prayers and in our good living by His help and His grace, concentrating our powers on Him until we love, in fullness of joy, Him whom we seek; that is, Jesus.

—Julian of Norwich (ca. 1342–1423), *The Revelation of Divine Love in Sixteen Showings*[3]

---

sionaries of Charity, but then was in profound spiritual darkness for virtually the last half century of her life.[2] Nevertheless,
despite her interior dryness she prayed for two hours every day.

Backed up by great spiritual writers such as Julian of Norwich (ca. 1342–1423) and John of the Cross (1542–91), C. S.
Lewis explains why the Lord sometimes lets us feel that he
has abandoned us. In *The Screwtape Letters*, Lewis has the
master devil explain that our prayer fluctuates between peaks
and troughs and that God especially values our prayers made
when we feel dry. Screwtape says that God in his efforts to get
permanent possession of a soul

> relies on the troughs even more than the peaks . . . One must
> face the fact that all the talk about His love for men, and
> His service being perfect freedom is not (as one would gladly
> believe) mere propaganda, but appalling truth. He really does
> want to fill the universe with a lot of loathsome little replicas
> of Himself—creatures whose life, on its miniature scale, will
> be qualitatively like His own, not because he absorbed them,
> but because their wills freely conform to His . . .
>
> He will set them off with communications of His presence
> which, though faint, seem great to them, with emotional sweet-
> ness, and easy conquest over temptation. But He never allows
> this state of affairs to last long. Sooner or later He withdraws,
> if not in fact, at least from their conscious experience, all those
> supports and incentives. He leaves the creature to stand up on
> its own legs—to carry out from the will alone duties which
> have lost all relish. It is during such trough periods, much more
> than during the peak periods, that it is growing into the sort
> of creature He wants it to be. Hence the prayers offered in the
> state of dryness are those which please Him best.[4]

So when dryness persists, I keep in mind that intimacy with God does not only mean feeling close to God or being attracted to him. In addition to a devotional component, intimacy with the Lord also involves remaining loyal to him. Scripture teaches that the Lord stays close to those who follow his ways. "Whoever holds to my commandments and keeps them," said Jesus, "is the one who loves me; and whoever loves me will be loved by my Father, and I shall love him and reveal myself to him" (John 14:21 NJB). When I don't feel like praying I do it anyway, professing my love and obedience as a disciple. The dryness does not magically disappear, but I know that the Lord draws near.

## Doubt

A severe case of doubt once stopped me from praying for the better part of a year. I have already told how failing my master's exam occasioned my angry turning from God to a disastrous period of willful self-reliance.[5] I doubted that God listened to my prayers or that he even cared for me, so I cut off communication with him. It took the prayers and interventions of my wife and friends to get me back on track. That dark experience had a bright side. The misery it caused me inoculated me against recurrences of doubting God since then when things have hit bottom.

Dealing with doubt involves identifying its cause and applying appropriate antidotes. Here are some sources of doubt and prescriptions for handling it.

*Unanswered prayer.* When we have asked God to heal us or resolve some difficulty and nothing seems to happen, we may think that he doesn't listen to prayer or even that he doesn't

134

care. To counteract doubt rooted in unanswered prayer, we must balance our expectations with trust, the two-sided approach that I recommended in an earlier chapter.[6] We should expect God to intervene in our lives, relieving our pain, resolving our problems, and delivering us from evil. But we cannot presume to pray away all problems. We must trust that whatever God does or does not do for us will be most loving, merciful, and just. We know that he hears our prayers but may delay his answer, just as he heard Christ's plea at Gethsemane, but answered it only after his passion at his resurrection.

*Why me?* When bad things happen to us, we are tempted to blame God and react with doubts about his love for us. Financial problems, job loss, broken relationships, poor health, the death of someone we love—all such situations may make us wonder, "Why me, Lord?" We may react by behaving badly. Believe me, I know the feeling and the reaction.

My friend George Cope, the pastor of Calvary Assembly in Winter Park, Florida, says that when we are hurting, we should ask "What?" not "Why?" He explains that God does not cause evil things, but he may allow them as occasions of grace. When something bad hits us, we must ask, "What good will God bring out of this?" For example, my humiliation and grief over failing my master's exam occasioned my being renewed in the Holy Spirit. The Lord brought a great good for me out of what seemed to me to be the worst of circumstances.

Expecting the Lord to transform the bad things that happen to us will not eliminate the pain. Staying connected to him in prayer, however, will give us the strength and confidence to get through it. Julian of Norwich says that the Lord revealed to her that since Jesus fixed Adam's sin, the worst of all evils, we can expect him to fix all the lesser ones that we experience.

---

**Standing Firm**

I've had these temptations for forty-one years now—do you think I'm going to give up after all this time? Absolutely not. I'll never stop hoping in God . . .

Most often, there is a confused sort of strife in my soul. Between feelings of being plunged into impenetrable darkness that I am powerless to do anything about, I have a kind of spiritual nausea that tempts me to give up trying . . . On the one hand, I am caught between the excruciating pain, and on the other hand, my love for our holy Faith that is so deep I would die rather than deny the least article of it.

If I can keep from offending God in spite of all this, then I am content with whatever it may please him to allow me to suffer, even if I must suffer for the rest of my life. I want only to do it knowing that he wants me to, and that in suffering I am being faithful to him.

—From a letter of Jane de Chantal (1572–1641), in *Saint Jeanne de Chantal: Noble Lady, Holy Woman*[7]

---

She wrote, "Because of the tender love our good Lord has for all those who shall be saved, He gives comfort readily and sweetly, assuring us, 'It is true that sin is the cause of all this pain, but all shall be well, all shall be well, and all manner of things shall be well . . . For since I have made well the greatest harm, then it is My will that you know thereby that I shall make well all that is less.'"[8]

*Darkness.* St. John of the Cross (1542–91) suggested in his books that God may allow pray-ers to experience periods of darkness to accomplish something in them that cannot be achieved in any other manner. Some great saints felt abandoned by God for many years and in their agony came to be mirrors of Christ in their character and service. For example, while enduring an impenetrable darkness for forty years, St. Jane de Chantal (1572–1641) revived the spirits of hundreds of seventeenth-century women with her wisdom and encouragement. In our own day Mother Teresa brought light out of her experience of darkness for the materially and spiritually poor and dying of the world.

The example of saints like these gives us hope when doubt shrouds our souls with gloom. They bore their suffering, knowing that Jesus himself suffered with them and supported them. As the writer of Hebrews says, "For the suffering he himself passed through while being put to the test enables him to help others when they are being put to the test" (Heb. 2:18 NJB). The faithfulness of Jane de Chantal and Mother Teresa enabled them to bear good fruit in their service. If darkness engulfs us, we too can count on the Lord to accompany us, support us, and give us the grace to serve others with love.

## Strengthened for Faithfulness

I have learned to take some steps to help me stay faithful to daily prayer. I keep in mind that prayer is God's gift to me. He gives me the grace to converse with him and expects me to respond. Most of the time I can communicate freely with him, but I want to be prepared to deal with distractions, dryness, or doubts when they come. So I strengthen my heart for fidelity by modeling my prayer on themes that weave through the psalms. The opening verses of Psalm 105 capture most of these:

> O give thanks to the LORD, call on his name,
>> make known his deeds among the peoples.
> Sing to him, sing praises to him;
>> tell of all his wonderful works.
> Glory in his holy name;
>> let the hearts of those who seek the LORD rejoice.
> Seek the LORD and his strength;

seek his presence continually.
Remember the wonderful works he has done,
his miracles, and the judgments he uttered.
—Psalms 105:1–5

As I pray psalms like this one, I take time to perform the actions proclaimed. I *remember* all the wonders the Lord has done for me and the words he has spoken to me. I *thank* him for everything, including birth, eternal life, family, friends, gifts, and especially forgiveness. I take time to *sing* his praises as best I can. I *seek* him, his strength, and his presence. I *rejoice* that I can participate in the loving relationships of the divine family. I *call* on his name and *glory* in it by meditating on the sign of the cross. And I decide that I will *make known* his wonderful works for me to others at my earliest opportunity. I do some or all of these things at prayer every morning and I'm convinced that they assure my faithfulness.

Think
- Have you decided to schedule fifteen minutes of prime time daily for prayer? Have you been faithful to daily prayer?
- What obstacles to prayer do you experience? Distractions? Dryness? Doubts?
- How do you handle these obstacles?

Pray

Take fifteen minutes to pray and consider the following:

- What steps must I take to be faithful to daily prayer?
- Make a list of the actions that occur to you and prioritize them.

Act
- Implement the actions on your list one at a time over the next two months.

# 12

## Prayer and Christian Growth

One night in the spring of 1939, Thomas Merton (1915–68) and poet Robert Lax (1915–2000), his Jewish friend, were walking along Sixth Avenue in Manhattan. Lax surprised Merton by asking out of the blue, "What do you want to be?" Merton, not wanting to appear shallow by saying "a writer" or "a philosophy teacher," correctly regarded the question as spiritual. "I don't know," he said. "I guess I want to be a good Catholic."

Lax rejected this answer. "What you should say," he told Merton, "is that you want to be a saint."

"How do you expect me to become a saint?" Merton asked.

"By wanting to," said Lax. "All that is necessary to be a saint is to want to be one. Don't you believe that God will make you what he created you to be, if you will consent to let him do it? All you have to do is desire it."[1]

Lax was right. God wants to make us all saints. Not that he intends that we should be formally canonized by the Catholic Church. But Scripture indicates that he always planned to sanctify us. For example, when Jesus described the scene of the final judgment he revealed that making saints was God's purpose in creation. To some people he would say, "Come, you that are blessed by my Father, inherit the kingdom prepared for you from the foundation of the world" (Matt. 25:34). To "inherit the kingdom" meant receiving eternal life; "the foundation of the world" referred to the creation of the universe. Jesus was telling us that his Father decided to create the universe so he could bestow eternal life on human beings who desired it.

So don't be too quick to latch on to Merton's initial reaction, which was a version of "Who, me be a saint? I could never be good enough." That's an excuse, not a reason. It's the fruit of a false humility that could cause us to miss a divine opportunity. Nobody, not even a great saint like Thérèse of Lisieux or Francis of Assisi, is good enough to become a saint. We must resist our inclination to regard saints as extraordinary human beings, made of better material than the rest of us.

Since 1997 I have read more than 350 lives of saints and can say with certainty that not one was good to begin with. All were ordinary people like you and me, who suffered with flaws, struggled against evil tendencies, and stumbled into sin. What sets saints apart is not some preternatural excellence, but a decision to say yes to God's call to sanctity. For example, Thérèse of Lisieux says she made a choice to be a saint when she was three years old. Francis of Assisi announced his intention to be a saint at age nineteen. God honored their decisions and made them saints. He wants to do the same for us, if we will only make the choice.

## Becoming like Christ

God makes us holy by uniting us with Christ so that we can become like him. The vehicle that he uses to ignite this revolutionary change in us is our baptism. There in the waters of the sacrament we die with Christ to our old nature and rise with him to put on a new and divine nature. Speaking of his baptismal transformation, Paul says, "I have been crucified with Christ; and it is no longer I who live, but it is Christ who lives in me. And the life I now live in the flesh I live by faith in the Son of God, who loved me and gave himself for me" (Gal. 2:20). In this way God transforms us from the inside out, as C. S. Lewis says, making us into "little Christs."[2]

---

### Becoming Little Christs

The church exists for nothing else but to draw men into Christ, to make them little Christs. If they are not doing that, all the cathedrals, clergy, missions, sermons, even the Bible itself, are simply a waste of time. God became Man for no other purpose. It is even doubtful, you know, that the whole universe was created for any other purpose . . .

The command *Be ye perfect* is not idealistic gas. Nor is it a command to do the impossible. He is going to make us into creatures that can obey that command. He said (in the Bible) that we were "gods" and he is going to make good his words. If we let him—for we can prevent him if we choose—he will make the feeblist and filthiest of us into a god or goddess, [a] dazzling, radiant, immortal creature, pulsating all through with such energy and love as we cannot now imagine which reflects back to God perfectly . . . his own boundless power and delight and goodness. The process will be long and in parts very painful; but that is what we are in for. Nothing less. He meant what he said . . .

The more we get what we now call "ourselves" out of the way and let him take us over, the more truly ourselves we become . . . Your real new self . . . will not come as long as you are looking for it. It will come when you are looking for him.

—C. S. Lewis (1898–1963), *Mere Christianity*[3]

---

Our transformation into Christ occurs gradually, almost imperceptibly. We advance in Christlikeness especially at prayer, when we sense his nearness, hear his voice in our thoughts, and discern his will for us. St. Catherine of Siena (1347–80), the great fourteenth-century mystic, says that by continual humble prayer "the soul is united to God, following in the footsteps of Christ crucified, and through desire and affection and the union of love he makes of her another himself. So Christ seems to have meant when he said, 'If you will love me and keep my word, I will show myself to you, and you will be *one thing* with me and I with you'"[4] (see John 14:21–23).

That's what happened to Father Larry Richards when he was an unbelieving teenager. Fr. Richards, now a nationally renowned evangelist, says that at seventeen he did not even know, let alone believe, that God existed. One day in English class he read *Our Town*, a play about death by Thornton Wilder

---

**The Transforming Power of Prayer**

This power, the grace of the Spirit, is not something we can merit or achieve, but only receive as pure gift. God's love can only unleash its power when it is allowed to change us from within. We have to let it break through the hard crust of our indifference, our spiritual weariness, our blind conformity to the spirit of this age. Only then can we let it ignite our imagination and shape our deepest desires. That is why prayer is so important: daily prayer, private prayer in the quiet of our hearts and before the Blessed Sacrament, and liturgical prayer in the heart of the Church. Prayer is pure receptivity to God's grace, love in action, communion with the Spirit who dwells within us, leading us, through Jesus, in the Church, to our heavenly Father. In the power of his Spirit, Jesus is always present in our hearts, quietly waiting for us to be still with him, to hear his voice, to abide in his love, and to receive "power from on high," enabling us to be salt and light for our world (see Luke 24:49; Matt. 5:13–14).

— Pope Benedict XVI, World Youth Day homily, Sydney, Australia, July 20, 2008

(1897–1975), and realized in terror that he too was going to die. That harrowing fear drove him to his knees.

From that day he went often to the Church of the Epiphany in downtown Pittsburgh, and appealed to God. "God, do you exist? Do you care?" he would ask. After six months of his humble seeking, God came to him. "Finally," he says, "one day sitting there in church . . . kneeling, seeking and just crying out to God, I came to know that Jesus Christ was real and that he was God. How did Christ reveal himself to me? As I knelt there I became aware that I was not alone. Here before me was the God of the universe, who had always been there but I was so focused on myself that I could not see him. I did not hear his voice . . . but I felt his presence. A Real Presence. A Presence that keeps everything in existence! I remember looking at him and saying, 'Lord, whatever you want I will do.' So at seventeen years old sitting in the Church of the Epiphany I heard the Lord tell me: 'I want you to be a priest.' My life was about to change—a lot!"[5] And change it did, as the teen matured and became, in Catherine of Siena's words, "one thing" with Christ.

## Gradual Change

I also desire to become a "little Christ,"—"one thing" with him—but I know I still have a long way to go. I feel that I take two steps forward, and one step back. I grow a little bit more like the Lord, then I fall back into a habitual flaw or a familiar sin, or I renege on a decision to follow him more closely.

Last year, for example, I was asked to write about the gifts of the Spirit for our parish newsletter. These gifts first appear in Isaiah and include reverence for the heart and wisdom for the mind (see Isa. 11:2 and chap. 4, p. 50). Writing the article prompted me to pray daily for more reverence and wisdom. Now I begin more prayer times with a sense of reverent awe—two steps forward—but then drift into "urgent" distractions about the day's business—a step back. As I prayed for wisdom, I recently sensed the Lord leading me to look for opportunities to speak to my adult children about the Christian life. I have been talking to one son about spending more time at prayer and to another son about priorities. That's two steps forward. I am missing more chances than I am seizing—one step back. But I have decided to keep at it.

A decade ago I began to make the sign of the cross with more faith, and that ancient prayer has also helped me grow in Christ. I explained in a previous book the ways that it strengthens me.[6] Tracing the cross over my breast brings me into the Lord's presence and renews the baptismal graces that empower me for Christian living. Most of all, each time I make the sign of the cross I affirm my decision to give myself to Christ as his disciple—to follow him, to become like him, and to work with him to continue his earthly ministry.

**Signs of Change**

Whene'r across this sinful flesh of mine
I draw the Holy Sign,
All good thoughts stir within me,
and renew
Their slumbering strength divine;
Till there springs up a courage high
and true
To suffer and to do.

—John Henry Newman (1801–90),
"The Sign of the Cross"[7]

Saint Paul says that we must put our evil habits to death and crucify the passions that lead us to sin (see Rom. 8:13; Gal. 5:24; Col. 3:5). I use the sign of the cross to prepare me to trade my bad behaviors for good ones. Frequently I sign myself, praying, "Lord, I am putting my habit of anger to death on this cross. Today, let me replace my irritability with patience." Or I may say, "With this sign I kill my rash judgments. Let me view my neighbors' actions with care and mercy." Then throughout the day, when something does not go my way or someone acts in a way that seems wrong, I am more apt to respond in a Christlike manner.

A few years ago I was speaking to a priest friend about some challenges I was facing, and he made a penetrating observation about me. I sensed that God was speaking through him. He said, "You like to keep things under control, don't you?" I doubted that anything I had said had given him a clue about my predominant flaw. "How do you know that?" I asked. "Oh, by the way you hold your head when you talk," he said, making a lame cover-up for discernment that I believe came from the Lord. His perceptive observation has preoccupied my self-examination for a long time. It has driven me to pray daily about the core of my sinfulness. I have learned that my compulsion to stay in control influences my need to be right, my reluctance to accept correction, my rushing to judgment about people, and my irritability when things don't go my way. I pray daily for the grace to surrender my independent streak to God. I am striving to behave in ways that break my "control-freak" tendencies. I try not to insist on my view in discussions that could become arguments. When little things go wrong and inconvenience me, I fight impatience as best I can. I am also attempting to withhold judgment on others. I win about half the time.

## The Promise and Power of Daily Prayer

Performing all the spiritual disciplines enables us to respond to the graces that advance our growth in Christ. These essential practices include prayer, Scripture study, fasting, evangelization, and care for the poor. Daily prayer plays a special role among these disciplines. It opens us to the Holy Spirit who instigates the other activities and directs us in doing God's work. By immersing us in the Lord's presence, our prayer occasions our becoming little Christs. We become like him because we live in his presence, just as children become like their parents because they live with them.

Faithfulness to daily prayer promises to create opportunities for us to be formed in the character of Christ that we see displayed in the Gospels. For example, we will find ourselves beginning to conform to the Beatitudes, which depict Christ's own behaviors. We will be more inclined to trust God, to meekly endure suffering, to stand up for what is right, and to show mercy (see Matt. 5:1–11). As we spend time with Christ in prayer, we will also notice that we are gradually adopting his dispositions—his humility before the Father, his compassion for the suffering, his hatred for evil, and his eagerness to share the good news.

Thus, we will experience the power of God's love in our daily prayer. It will open us to fulfilling God's purpose in creating us by letting him make us into his saints.

Think
- What do you think is the purpose of your life?
- Has it occurred to you that God made you to be a saint?
- In what ways could prayer advance your growth as a Christian?
- Which of your behaviors should you ask the Lord to help you change?
- Which characteristics of Christ do you most need to reproduce in your life?

Pray

Take fifteen minutes to prayerfully consider the following:

- What would it mean for me to decide to be a saint?
- Am I willing to let the Holy Spirit make me more like Christ?
- What is the core of my sinfulness? What must I do to overcome it?

Act
- Decide to be a saint.
- Open yourself in prayer to the Holy Spirit. Invite him to come into your heart afresh and advance your transformation in Christ.
- Make or renew your commitment to daily prayer and observe it faithfully. Expect the Lord to gradually make you into a little Christ.

# Bibliography

Binz, Stephen J. *Conversing with God in Scripture*. Ijamsville, MD: The Word Among Us Press, 2008.

Brother Lawrence. *The Practice of the Presence of God and The Spiritual Maxims*. New York: Cosimo Classics, 2006.

Brown, Raymond E. *New Testament Reading Guide: The Gospel of John and The Johannine Epistles*. Collegeville, MN: Liturgical Press, 1960.

*Butler's Lives of the Saints: New Full Edition*. Edited by David Hugh Farmer. Collegeville, MN: Liturgical Press, 1999.

Carroll, Warren H. "The Conversion of Ireland." www.catholic culture.org/culture/library/view.cfm?recnum=101.

*Catherine of Siena: The Dialogue*. Translated by Suzanne Noffke, OP. The Classics of Western Spirituality. New York: Paulist Press, 1980.

*Christian Readings*. New York: The Catholic Book Publishing Company, 1972.

*The Collected Works of St. John of the Cross*. Translated by Kiernan Kavenaugh, OCD, and Otilio Rodriguez, OCD. Washington, DC: Institute of Carmelite Studies, 1973.

De'Liguori, St. Alphonsus. *How to Converse Continually and Familiarly with God*. Translated by L. X. Aubin, CSSR. Boston: St. Paul Editions, 1963.

De Sales, St. Francis. *Introduction to the Devout Life*. Translated and edited by John K. Ryan. New York: Image Books, 1989.

Englebert, Omer. *St. Francis of Assisi: A Biography*. Ann Arbor, MI: Servant Books, 1979.

Ghezzi, Bert. *Living the Sacraments*. Cincinnati, OH: Servant Books, 2011.

———. *The Sign of the Cross*. Chicago: Loyola Press, 2004.

Green, Thomas H., SJ. *Opening to God*. Rev. ed. Notre Dame, IN: Ave Maria Press, 2006.

Groeschel, Benedict, CFR, and Bert Ghezzi. *Everyday Encounters with God*. Ijamsville, MD: The Word Among Us Press, 2008.

Guitton, George, SJ. *Perfect Friend: The Life of Blessed Claude la Columbière*. Translated by William J. Young, SJ. St. Louis: B. Herder Book Company, 1956.

*The Hymnbook of the Anglican Church of Canada and the United Church of Canada*. Toronto: Cooper and Beatty, 1971.

Kempis, Thomas à. *The Imitation of Christ*. Edited by Harold C. Gardiner, SJ. Translated by Richard Whitford. New York: Image Books, 1989.

Lewis, C. S. *Mere Christianity*. New York: Macmillan, 1968.

———. *The Screwtape Letters and Screwtape Proposes a Toast*. New York: Macmillan, 1970.

———. *The Weight of Glory and Other Addresses*. New York: Macmillan, 1949.

Mangan, David. *God Loves You and There's Nothing You Can Do about It*. Cincinnati: Servant Books, 2008.

Mansfield, Patti. *As By a New Pentecost*. Steubenville, OH: Franciscan University Press, 1992.

Martin, George. *Bringing the Gospel of Mark to Life*. Huntington, IN: Our Sunday Visitor, 2013.

———. *Bringing the Gospel of Luke to Life*. Huntington, IN: Our Sunday Visitor, 2011.

———. *Praying with Jesus*. Chicago: Loyola Press, 2000.

———. *Reading God's Word Today*. Huntington, IN: Our Sunday Visitor, 2009.

Merton, Thomas. *Contemplative Prayer*. Garden City, NY: Image Books, 1971.

———. *The Seven Storey Mountain*. New York: Harcourt, Brace, 1948.

Miller, Patrick D., Jr. "In Praise and Thanksgiving." http://theologytoday.ptsem.edu/jul1988/v45-2-article3.htm.

Montague, George T., SM. *Holy Spirit, Make Your Home in Me*. Ijamsville, MD: The Word Among Us Press, 2008.

*Mother Teresa: Come Be My Light.* Edited with a Commentary by Brian Kolodiejchuk, MC. New York: Doubleday, 2007.

Nee, Watchman. *The Normal Christian Life.* Fort Washington, PA: Christian Literature Crusade, 1969.

Nouwen, Henri J. M. *With Open Hands.* Notre Dame, IN: Ave Maria Press, 2005.

*The Office of Readings According to the Roman Rite.* Translated by the International Commission on English in the Liturgy. Boston: Daughters of St. Paul, 1983.

Ranaghan, Kevin and Dorothy. *Catholic Pentecostals.* New York: Paulist Press, 1969.

Ravier, Andre, SJ. *Saint Jeanne de Chantal: Noble Lady, Holy Woman.* San Francisco: Ignatius Press, 1989.

*The Revelation of Divine Love in Sixteen Showings: Made to Dame Julian of Norwich.* Translated by M. L. del Mastro. Liguori, MO: Liguori Publications, 1994.

Rolheiser, Ronald, OMI. "Deeper Things Under the Surface." January 29, 2006, www.ronrolheiser.com/columnarchive/archive_display.php?rec_id=63.

Sheed, Frank J. *A Map of Life.* San Francisco: Ignatius Press, 1994.

———. *Theology and Sanity.* San Francisco: Ignatius Press, 1978.

———. *Theology for Beginners.* Ann Arbor, MI: Servant Books, 1981.

Squire, Aelred. *Aelred of Rievaulx: A Study.* London: SPCK, 1973.

Storey, William G. *A Catholic Book of Hours and Other Devotions.* Chicago: Loyola Press, 2007.

Wilkerson, David. *The Cross and the Switchblade.* New York: Spire Books, 1963.

Willard, Dallas. *The Divine Conspiracy.* San Francisco: HarperSanFrancisco, 1997.

Yancey, Philip. *Prayer: Does It Make Any Difference?* Grand Rapids: Zondervan, 2006.

# Acknowledgments

My friend, Deacon Henry Libersat, jokes that in writing my books I always borrow from others. The core of truth in that observation makes it funny. And as always I am indebted to many friends and associates who contributed to this book and who have made it better. So I extend hearty thanks to James Manney, Susan Manney, George Martin, Patricia Mitchell, Nancy Sabbag, and Brandon Vogt.

My mentor, William G. Storey, read the manuscript fearing that I might praise him too highly, but I did not praise him enough. Thanks, Bill, for everything.

I am especially grateful for the friendship, encouragement, and direction of Joseph Durepos, who more than anyone else has helped me grow as a writer and established me as an author. Thanks, too, to the publishing teams at Brazos and The Word Among Us Press for their excellent work and support.

And finally to Mary Lou, my longsuffering wife, who must spend part of her daily prayer asking for forbearance of her intensely preoccupied husband—I give my love and gratitude.

# Notes

1. L. X. Aubin, CSSR, trans., *How to Converse Continually and Familiarly with God* (Boston: St. Paul Editions, 1963), 20–21, 44.

## Introduction

1. The Pew Research Center for People and the Press, April 10, 2001, http://people-press.org/report/?pageid=115.

2. "O most merciful redeemer, friend and brother, may I know thee more clearly, love thee more dearly, and follow thee more nearly" quoted in David Hugh Farmer, ed., *Butler's Lives of the Saints: New Full Edition* (Collegeville, MN: Liturgical Press, 1999), April, 18.

3. Thomas H. Green, SJ, *Opening to God*, rev. ed. (Notre Dame, IN: Ave Maria Press, 2006), 36.

## Chapter 1  Adventures in Daily Prayer

1. Dallas Willard, *The Divine Conspiracy* (San Francisco: HarperSanFrancisco, 1997), 65.

2. C. S. Lewis, *The Screwtape Letters and Screwtape Proposes a Toast* (New York: Macmillan, 1970), 22.

3. Archbishop Stephen Langton of Canterbury, *Veni Sancte Spiritus*, trans. John Webster Grant. Used by permission of Professor Phyllis Airhart.

4. William G. Storey, *A Catholic Book of Hours and Other Devotions* (Chicago: Loyola Press, 2007). Readers who want to explore praying the hours may also consider Phyllis Tickle's wonderful *The Divine Hours* in 3 vols. (New York: Doubleday, 2000–2001), and numerous derivatives. See www.phyllistickle.com.

5. Exposition on Psalm 118 by St. Ambrose (339–97) in *The Office of Readings According to the Roman Rite*, trans. International

Commission on English in the Liturgy (Boston: Daughters of St. Paul, 1983), 866–67 (emphasis in original).

### Chapter 2  Giving Ourselves to God

1. Ronald Rolheiser, OMI, "Deeper Things Under the Surface," January 29, 2006, www.ronrolheiser.com/columnarchive/archive_display .php?rec_id=63.

2. George Martin, *Praying with Jesus* (Chicago: Loyola Press, 2000), 49–50.

### Chapter 3  Living in God's Presence

1. See, for example, St. Francis de Sales, *Introduction to the Devout Life*, ed. and trans. John K. Ryan (New York: Image Books, 1989), 82.

2. Dallas Willard, *The Divine Conspiracy* (San Francisco: HarperSanFrancisco, 1997), 74.

3. Frank J. Sheed (1897–1981), *Theology and Sanity* (San Francisco: Ignatius Press, 1978), 64–65; and idem., *Theology for Beginners* (Ann Arbor, MI: Servant Books, 1981), 19.

4. Willard, *Divine Conspiracy*, 67.

5. Benedict Groeschel, CFR, and Bert Ghezzi, *Everyday Encounters with God* (Ijamsville, MD: The Word Among Us Press, 2008), 8–9.

6. Brother Lawrence, *The Practice of the Presence of God and The Spiritual Maxims* (New York: Cosimo Classics, 2006), 19–20.

### Chapter 4  Praying in the Spirit

1. David Wilkerson, *The Cross and the Switchblade* (New York: Spire Books, 1963).

2. For more details about these events, see Patti Mansfield, *As By a New Pentecost* (Steubenville, OH: Franciscan University Press, 1992); and David Mangan, *God Loves You and There's Nothing You Can Do about It* (Cincinnati: Servant Books, 2008).

3. George T. Montague, SM, *Holy Spirit, Make Your Home in Me* (Ijamsville, MD: The Word Among Us Press, 2008), 131, 133.

4. *On the Holy Spirit*, a catechetical instruction by St. Cyril of Jerusalem (ca. 315–86) in *The Office of Readings According to the Roman Rite*, trans. International Commission on English in the Liturgy (Boston: Daughters of St. Paul, 1983), 629–30.

5. *Veni, Creator Spiritus*, attributed to Rabanus Maurus (776–856). Adapted from *Liturgy of the Hours*, trans. Anon. (New York: Catholic Book Publishing Company, 1976), II, 1011.

6. International Catholic Charismatic Renewal Services, www.iccrs .org/CCR%20worldwide.htm.

## Chapter 5 Praying with Thanksgiving

1. *The Revelation of Divine Love in Sixteen Showings: Made to Dame Julian of Norwich*, trans. M. L. del Mastro (Liguori, MO: Liguori Publications, 1994), 123–24.

2. Patrick D. Miller Jr., "In Praise and Thanksgiving," *Theology Today*, July 1988, http://theologytoday.ptsem.edu/jul1988/v45-2 -article3.htm.

3. Quoted in George Guitton, SJ, *Perfect Friend: The Life of Blessed Claude la Columbière*, trans. William J. Young, SJ (St. Louis: B. Herder Book Company, 1956), 326 (slightly adapted by the author).

4. Miller, "In Praise and Thanksgiving" (emphasis in original).

## Chapter 6 Praying with Scripture

1. Vatican Council II, Dogmatic Constitution on Divine Revelation, *Dei Verbum*, 21, www.vatican.va/archive/hist_councils/ ii_vatican_council.

2. Raymond E. Brown, *New Testament Reading Guide: The Gospel of John and the Johannine Epistles* (Collegeville, MN: Liturgical Press, 1960) identifies the translation as "Bible Text Copyright © 1952 by the Confraternity of Christian Doctrine."

3. St. Bonaventure (ca. 1218–74), *Breviloquium Prologue*, 2–5, in *Christian Readings* (New York: Catholic Book Publishing Company, 1972), I, 217.

4. For an excellent contemporary explanation of *lectio divina*, see Stephen J. Binz, *Conversing with God in Scripture* (Ijamsville, MD: The Word Among Us Press, 2008). Beginners and experienced Bible readers will find these books by George Martin helpful aids to praying with Scripture: *Reading God's Word Today* (Huntington, IN: Our Sunday Visitor, 2009); *Bringing the Gospel of Luke to Life* (2011) and *Bringing the Gospel of Mark to Life* (2013), both published by Our Sunday Visitor, Huntington, IN.

5. Watchman Nee, *The Normal Christian Life* (Fort Washington, PA: Christian Literature Crusade, 1969), 43.

6. St. Augustine, a letter to Proba, in *The Office of Readings According to the Roman Rite,* trans. International Commission on English in the Liturgy (Boston: Daughters of St. Paul, 1983), 1170.

7. *Conferences of John Cassian* (ca. 360–433), 10, *Nicene and Post-Nicene Fathers*, Series 2, Vol. 11.

8. Augustine, letter to Proba, *Office of Readings*, 1173.

Chapter 7  Listening to God

1. See chap. 3.

2. For a discussion and examples of God's communicating to us in our daily experiences, see Benedict Groeschel, CFR, and Bert Ghezzi, *Everyday Encounters with God* (Ijamsville, MD: The Word Among Us Press, 2008).

3. Thomas Merton, *Contemplative Prayer* (Garden City, NY: Image Books, 1971), 41.

4. Omer Englebert, *St. Francis of Assisi: A Biography* (Ann Arbor, MI: Servant Books, 1979), 33–34.

5. C. S. Lewis, *The Weight of Glory and Other Addresses* (New York: Macmillan, 1949), 14–15.

6. Thomas à Kempis, *The Imitation of Christ*, ed. Harold C. Gardiner, SJ, trans. Richard Whitford (New York: Image Books, 1989), 75, 104–5.

Chapter 8  Relying on God

1. A papal bull is a particular type of legal document or charter issued by a pope. It is named after the "bulla" or seal that was appended to the end to authenticate it.

2. Rev. Robert D. Lunsford, "Through This Holy Anointing—Then and Now," *God's Word Today*, August 1980, 43.

3. Philip Yancey, *Prayer: Does It Make Any Difference?* (Grand Rapids: Zondervan, 2006), 249, 257.

4. Ibid., 259–66.

5. Bert Ghezzi, *Living the Sacraments* (Cincinnati OH: Servant Books, 2011), 98–99.


Chapter 9  Praying for Others

1. The Cursillo movement originated in Majorca, Spain, in the 1940s with the purpose of engaging men in the mission activities of the Roman Catholic Church. The movement arrived in the United States around 1965. In this country Cursillo weekends are also offered for women.

2. Pope Paul VI (1897–1978), *Evangelii Num Ciandi* (*Evangelization in the Modern World*), December 8, 1975, 21–22, www.vatican .va/holy_father/paul_vi/apost_exhortations.

3. Learn more about this ministry at www.fraternus.net.


Chapter 10  Praying with Others

1. Frank J. Sheed (1897–1981), *A Map of Life* (San Francisco: Ignatius Press, 1994), 61–63 (emphasis in original).

2. Pope Pius XII (1876–1958), *Mystici Corporis Christi*, June 29, 1943, 55, www.vatican.va/holy_father/pius_xii/encyclicals/documents/ hf_p-xii_enc_2906943_mystici-corporis-christi_en.html.

3. Aelred of Rievaulx (1110–67), *Spiritual Friendship*, cited in and translated by Aelred Squire, *Aelred of Rievaulx: A Study* (London: SPCK, 1973), 49–50.

4. On the Cursillo, see chap. 9, p. 107.

5. See Brandon's blog at www.brandonvogt.com.

## Chapter 11  Faithfulness to Prayer

1. *The Confession of St. Patrick*, trans. Warren H. Carroll, in "The Conversion of Ireland," at www.catholicculture.org/culture/library/view.cfm?recnum=101.

2. See *Mother Teresa: Come Be My Light* (New York: Doubleday, 2007) for her moving testimony about that darkness.

3. *The Revelation of Divine Love in Sixteen Showings: Made to Dame Julian of Norwich*, trans. M. L. del Mastro (Liguori, MO: Liguori Publications, 1994), 123.

4. C. S. Lewis, *The Screwtape Letters and Screwtape Proposes a Toast* (New York: Macmillan, 1970), 37–39.

5. See chap. 4, pp. 44–45.

6. Chap. 8, pp. 97–100.

7. From a letter of Jane de Chantal cited in André Ravier, SJ, *Saint Jeanne de Chantal: Noble Lady, Holy Woman* (San Francisco: Ignatius Press, 1989), 185–87.

8. *Revelation of Divine Love in Sixteen Showings*, 102, 105.

## Chapter 12  Prayer and Christian Growth

1. Thomas Merton, *The Seven Storey Mountain* (New York: Harcourt, Brace, 1948), 237–38.

2. C. S. Lewis, *Mere Christianity* (New York: Macmillan, 1968), 169.

3. Ibid., 169–70, 174–75, 189–90.

4. *Catherine of Siena: The Dialogue*, trans. Suzanne Noffke, OP, The Classics of Western Spirituality (New York: Paulist Press, 1980), 25 (emphasis added).

5. Fr. Larry Richards, *Be a Man* (San Francisco: Ignatius Press, 2009), 15.

6. Bert Ghezzi, *The Sign of the Cross* (Chicago: Loyola Press, 2004).

7. John Henry Newman, "The Sign of the Cross," in *A Victorian Anthology 1837–1895*, ed. Edmund Clarence Stedman (Bartleby.com, 2003).

## the WORD among us®
### The Spirit of Catholic Living

This book was published by The Word Among Us. Since 1981, The Word Among Us has been answering the call of the Second Vatican Council to help Catholic laypeople encounter Christ in the Scriptures.

The name of our company comes from the prologue to the Gospel of John and reflects the vision and purpose of all of our publications: to be an instrument of the Spirit, whose desire is to manifest Jesus' presence in and to the children of God. In this way, we hope to contribute to the Church's ongoing mission of proclaiming the gospel to the world so that all people would know the love and mercy of our Lord and grow ever more deeply in love with him.

Our monthly devotional magazine, *The Word Among Us*, features meditations on the daily and Sunday Mass readings, and currently reaches more than one million Catholics in North America and another half million Catholics in one hundred countries around the world. Our book division, The Word Among Us Press, publishes numerous books, Bible studies, and pamphlets that help Catholics grow in their faith.

To learn more about who we are and what we publish, log on to our website at www.wau.org. There you will find a variety of Catholic resources that will help you grow in your faith.

# Embrace His Word, Listen to God . . .